This book should be returned to any branch of the
Lancashire County Library on or before the date

ENE

Great British Adventurers

This book is dedicated to the memory of
my grandparents.

For all the happy days you gave me.

Lo! Some we loved, the lov'liest and best
That Time and Fate of all their Vintage prest,
Have drunk their Cup a Round or two before,
And one by one crept silently to Rest.

From the translation of the *Rubáiyát of Omar Khayyám*
by Edward FitzGerald.

And it is also for C. A. Lovell and A. W. Smith:
Gware wheag yeo gware teag.
(Cornish language motto, for: 'Fair play is good play.')

Great British Adventurers

By Nicholas Storey

REMEMBER WHEN

First published in Great Britain in 2012 by
Remember When
an imprint of
Pen & Sword Books Ltd
47 Church Street
Barnsley
South Yorkshire
S70 2AS

ISBN: 978 1 84468 130 3

The right of Ni_____ of this work has
been asserted _____ t, Designs and
Pa_____88.

A CIP catalogue _____ e British Library.

Typeset by Mac Style, Driffield, East Yorkshire
Printed and bound in the UK by CPI Group (UK) Ltd, Croydon, CRO 4YY

Pen & Sword Books Ltd incorporates the Imprints of Pen & Sword Aviation,
Pen & Sword Family History, Pen & Sword Maritime, Pen & Sword Military,
Pen & Sword Discovery, Wharncliffe Local History, Wharncliffe True Crime,
Wharncliffe Transport, Pen & Sword Select, Pen & Sword Military Classics,
Leo Cooper, The Praetorian Press, Remember When, Seaforth Publishing
and Frontline Publishing.

For a complete list of Pen & Sword titles please contact
PEN & SWORD BOOKS LIMITED
47 Church Street, Barnsley, South Yorkshire, S70 2AS, England
E-mail: enquiries@pen-and-sword.co.uk
Website: www.pen-and-sword.co.uk

Contents

Acknowledgements

For looking over my draft chapter on Krystyna Skarbek-Granville, also known as Christine Granville (about whom there is much misinformation at large, even down to her date of birth), I thank Ron Nowicki. I also thank Ian Fleming biographer Andrew Lycett for his advice that he knows of no clear evidence that Ian Fleming even personally knew Krystyna, let alone had an affair with her, as is sometimes (sensationally) suggested. I thank too, Laurence Mann, of St Margaret's, Middlesex, and Dr Marcelo de Araujo, of Laranjeiras, Rio de Janeiro for looking over the whole draft at short notice and, as ever, making helpful suggestions. For any remaining errors I bear sole responsibility and all the opinions expressed are mine.

The illustrations, in subject order, as they appear in the book, are as follows:

Lady Hester Lucy Stanhope (1776–1839) from an original portrait of unknown provenance.

Sir James Brooke KCB, DCL (Oxon), White Rajah of Sarawak (1803–1868) from an original portrait by Francis Grant, RA.

Richard Lemon Lander (1804 –1834) from an original engraving of unknown provenance.

Mary Seacole (1805–1881) from an original portrait of unknown provenance.

Jane Elizabeth Digby (1807–1881) from an original portrait by Joseph Karl Stieler.

General Sir James Abbott KCB (1807–1896) from an original portrait by B. Baldwin.

Colonel John Whitehead Peard, 'Garibaldi's Englishman' (1811–1880) from a portrait of unknown provenance.

John William Colenso, 1st Anglican Bishop of Natal (1814–1883) from a photograph of unknown provenance.

Sir Richard Francis Burton KCMG (1821–1890) from an original portrait by Sir Frederick Leighton, RA, and a photograph of John Hanning Speke, 1827–1864, by Thomas Rodger.

Sir Thomas Johnstone Lipton Bart. KCVO (1850–1931) from a photograph of unknown provenance.

Emily Hobhouse (1860 –1926) from a photograph of unknown provenance.

Mary Henrietta Kingsley (1862–1900) from a photograph of unknown provenance.

Sir Francis Edward Younghusband KCSI, KCIE (1863–1942) from a photograph of unknown provenance.

Colonel Percy Harrison Fawcett (1867–1925) from a photograph by Pelecchuco and, in Fawcett's wake, (Robert) Peter Fleming OBE, (1907–1971), from a photograph of unknown provenance.

Gertrude Margaret Lowthian Bell CBE (1868–1926) from a photograph of unknown provenance.

George Herbert Leigh Mallory (1886–1924) from a photograph of unknown provenance.

Andrew Comyn Irvine, from a photograph of unknown provenance.

Dame Freya Madeline Stark DBE (ca.1893–1993) from a photograph of unknown provenance.

Sir Francis Charles Chichester KBE (1901–1972) from a photograph of unknown provenance.

Amy Johnson CBE (1902–1941) from a photograph of unknown provenance.

Gladys May Aylward (1902–1970) from a photograph of unknown provenance.

Krystyna Skarbek–Granville (Christine Granville) GM, OBE, Croix de Guerre (ca. 1908–1952) from a photograph of unknown provenance.

Sir Fitzroy Hew Royle Maclean Bart. KT, CBE (1911–1996) from a photograph of unknown provenance.

Noor-un-Nisa Inayat Khan, GC, MBE, Croix de Guerre (1914–1944) from a photograph of unknown provenance.

Tenzing Norgay GM (1914–1986) from the 'Mount Everest' photograph by Edmund Hillary.

Violette Reine Elizabeth Szabo GC, MBE, Croix de Guerre (1921–1945) from a photograph of unknown provenance.

Nicholas Storey,
Estado do Rio de Janeiro,
Brasil

Introduction

One equal temper of heroic hearts,
Made weak by time and fate, but strong in will
To strive, to seek, to find, and not to yield.
From Ulysses by Alfred, Lord Tennyson

About this Book

IN CHOOSING my particular adventurers I have had to find limits. The first has been to confine my selection to men and women who are (at least loosely), British, and even then, service and adoption have sometimes, as with Krystyna Skarbek-Granville (Christine Granville), taken the place of birth. I have chosen to ignore such things as competing national claims for Tenzing Norgay. The second limit I have set myself is generally to exclude heroic adventurers in battle, simply because there is (rightly), so much already written about them. I have, however, found place for certain (representative) female secret agents of the Second World War, whose acts (in voluntary service, beyond the call of simple duty), surely took them out of the arena of straightforward battle and into the realm of the most individual and courageous adventure. They were, moreover, the first modern, female British warriors, not just *on* the front line but *behind* it on the enemy's own turf, long, long before any calls on the grounds of 'sex equality' put modern women into battle.

The result of my decisions remains to be judged, but the overall objective has been to renew interest in the lives of some of our real heroes and heroines as representative of the many others that there are, in an age in which contemporary sporting and pop art 'heroes' dominate the news and provide the only readily evident 'inspiration', and also an age in which addiction to the computer screen nearly robs the young of memories and dreams of the high adventure of which ripping yarns are made.

The third limit is a limit of time. This speaks for itself, otherwise how would Drake and Raleigh, Clive of India, General Woolf and Captain Cook not have found their places? There have to be such limits. The final limit has been to exclude those who are widely famed already. What more is there to say in a book of this size, of General Gordon or Dr David Livingstone; of Charles Darwin, Captain Robert Falcon Scott, Captain Laurence Oates, Ernest Shackleton and T. E. 'Lawrence of Arabia', even though what has been said should never be forgotten? Moreover, although Sir Edmund Hillary is acknowledged as the first conqueror of Mount Everest, Tenzing Norgay was there with him. And what of George Mallory who, sometime before, had died, either going up or coming down?

I also cover the adventurous spirit in different degrees, just because it exists in different degrees: Sir Richard Burton's daring in making the Hajj pilgrimage is of quite a different kind from Sir Thomas Lipton's gentler adventures, in the nature of trade, in seeking out sources of, and markets for, tea. Yet each made a memorable contribution to the world.

As will be seen, some of my subjects were very, very good; some of them were very, very bad, and some, as I have come to know them better, I like very much. Some I do not like at all. Yet they all share the characteristics of originality, a sense of self-determination, unfettered by the diktats of Tin-Hitlers, a thirst for living, perseverance and persistence, and even defiance. Many of them showed bravery – some of them to a truly exceptional degree – and, I think, they all lived without the wish to have lived more quietly. In short, they shared a rage for life and yet also managed to see beyond themselves and the times in which they lived.

To those who might accuse me of having been at all obscure in my choices, I just plead that my purpose has been to bring back into ready remembrance, certain men and women, many of them not widely fêted now, who had great impact upon the accrual of knowledge of other peoples, their customs, their traditions and their countries, or who have striven, often against various obstacles (including the odds), to promote exploration and trade and, sometimes, even to preserve life and liberty for others. To the erudite who might say that I shed little new light, I plead, in mitigation of sentence, that my principal purpose has been to remind of worthy lives that might still stir our blood, and to bring them together as representatives of our adventurous people in one handy volume.

Finally, for the avoidance of doubt, the initials 'RGS' stand for 'Royal Geographical Society', and the initials 'SOE' stand for 'Special Operations Executive', which is first described in the entry for Krystyna Skarbek-Granville.

About Adventure and Adventurers

Adventure in Myth, Legend, Religion and History

Most of the great ancient myths and legends, as well as the stories associated with the prevalent world religions, involve high adventure.

Prometheus stole fire from Zeus and gave it to the mortals, ending in his being tied to a rock to be pecked at by an eagle.

Hercules had his twelve labours to atone for slaying his six sons: to slay the Nemean lion, slay the Lernaean Hydra, capture the Golden Hind of Artemis, capture the Erymanthian Boar, clean the Augean stables in a single day, slay the Stymphalian Birds, capture the Cretan Bull, steal the mare of Diomedes, take the girdle of Hippolyta, take the cattle of the monster Geryon, steal the apples of the Hesperides and, last but not least, capture Cerberus. Accomplishing them all, he was forgiven, and received the gift of immortality and Hebe as a bride. That is the ultimate adventure story.

The same may be said of Homer's *Iliad*, dealing with the quarrel between King Agamemnon and Achilles during the siege of Troy, and of the *Odyssey*, as well as dealing with the long journey home to Ithaca by Odysseus, all that had become of his wife Penelope and his son, *and* his (eventually victorious), struggle to reassert himself, against his wife's 'suitors', by virtue of the fact that only he, Odysseus, could bend his own bow and pierce a dozen axe heads with the arrows.

In the book of Exodus in the Old Testament, there is, most famously, Moses leading the Children of Israel out of Egypt, their long journey in the Wilderness (including the crossing of the Red Sea,) and the granting of the Covenant by God to mankind, followed by the establishment of the Promised Land.

The Arabs have stories such as *The Thousand Arabian Nights and One Night* (incidentally, as we shall see, translated by one of our adventurers, Sir Richard Burton).

In Sanskrit there are the great epics of ancient India, *Ramayana and Mahabharata*.

Ramayana is traditionally divided into several major *kāṇḍas* or books, that deal chronologically with the major events in the life of Rama: *Bāla Kāṇḍa, Ayodhya Kāṇḍa, Araṇḍya Kāṇḍa, Kishkindha Kāṇḍa, Sundara Kāṇḍa, Yuddha Kāṇḍa,* and *Uttara Kāṇḍa*. The *Bala Kāṇḍa* describes the birth of Rama, his childhood, and marriage to Sita. The *Ayodhya Kāṇḍa* describes the preparations for Rama's coronation and his exile in the forest. The third part, *Aranya Kāṇḍa*, describes the forest life of Rama and the kidnapping of Sita by the demon king, Ravana. The fourth book, *Kishkindha Kāṇḍa*, describes the meeting of Hanuman with Rama, the destruction of the vanara king, Bali, and the coronation of his younger brother Sugriva, on the throne of the kingdom of Kishkindha. The fifth book is *Sundara Kāṇḍa*, which narrates the heroism of Hanuman, his flight to Lanka, and his meeting with Sita. The sixth book, *Yuddha Kāṇḍa*, describes the battle between the armies of Rama and Ravana. The last book, *Uttara Kāṇḍa*, describes the birth of Lava and Kusha to Sita, their coronation on the throne of Ayodhya, and Rama's final departure from the world.

In *Mahabharata*, the core of the story is of a dynastic struggle for the throne of Hastinapura, the kingdom ruled by the Kuru clan. The two collateral branches of the family that participate in the strife are the Kaurava and the Pandava. Although the Kaurava is the senior branch of the family, Duryodhana, the eldest Kaurava, is younger than Yudhisthira, the eldest Pandava. Both Duryodhana and Yudhisthira claim to be first in line to inherit the throne.

The strife culminates in the great battle of Kurukshetra, in which the Pandavas are ultimately victorious. The battle produces conflicts of kinship and friendship, instances of family loyalty and duty taking precedence over what is objectively true and right.

The *Mahabharata* itself ends with the death of Krishna, the subsequent end of his dynasty, and the ascent of the Pandava brothers to heaven. It also marks the beginning of the Hindu age of Kali (Kali Yuga), the fourth and final age of mankind, in which all great values and noble ideas have crumbled, and man is heading toward the complete dissolution of truth, morality and all virtue.

Arshia Sattar states that the central themes of the *Mahabharata* (as well as of the *Ramayana*), are Krishna's and Rama's hidden divinity and their gradual evolution and revelation.

Buddhists have the quieter search for perfect enlightenment of the Lord Buddha himself under the holy olive tree, which is a grand adventure of the spirit.

Therefore, we can safely say that many of the world's great, ancient stories are stories of adventure of one sort or another and that they go on instructing and entertaining us.

The history books are also full of tales of real adventure, largely centring on the building-up and breaking-down of empires, from those of the Chinese dynasties, to the Roman Empire, the Macedonian Empire, the Mongol Empire, the Mughal Empire, the Russian Empire, the Spanish

Empire, the Brazilian Empire, the French Colonial Empires; scores of other empires, all through time and then, the largest (in territorial extent), of them all, the British Empire.

Adventure in Modern Fiction

Modern fiction is inspired and sustained to a remarkable extent by the spirit of adventure and the fundamental human liking for stories about it. Cervantes' *Don Quixote* is most clearly a tale of adventure. There is even something adventurous in Thomas de Quincey's *Confessions of an Opium Eater*. Adventure is certainly there in Henry Fielding's *Tom Jones* and *Moll Flanders*, and Dickens and Kipling bear rich lodes, especially *Nicholas Nickelby* from the one and *Kim* from the other.

J.R.R. Tolkien's *The Hobbit* and *The Lord of the Rings* are epic adventures and do seem to have kept a grip on the modern imagination.

Rider Haggard's stories, such as *She* and *King Solomon's Mines* (which are just two of many), grew in his imagination out of his own experiences in Africa and his interaction with the people he found there. Yet, while people continue to enjoy the stories (and watch the films), it does appear as though the majority of the human race is more and more reluctant to actually engage in adventure beyond the virtual kinds, and is increasingly drawn to televised kitchen-sink dramas and soap operas such as *EastEnders* and *Coronation Street* at one end, to *Downton Abbey* at the other.

W. E. Johns's wartime stories of the derring-do of Biggles and Worrals which my sister and I enjoyed as children, are probably on several 'banned' lists now because I suppose they harmlessly offend on too many points of strict, 'political correctness' – from the merits of smoking tobacco (undoubted) to the demerits of other national flags (considerable). I dare say that something similar goes for Enid Blyton's *Famous Five* books. But, all the while we know full well that real prejudices, on grounds of race and religion, and real hatreds too (on all sides), are boiling away beneath the surface of a society that pretends to be so 'right-on' but, in fact, has just turned recluse, muttering, 'Talk to the hand because the face ain't listenin.' It has not hidden its face 'amid a crowd of stars' but hidden its face in the 'telly' and the computer.

In the same way that the phenomenon of 'telly dinners', obligingly taken to children in their rooms as they undergo voluntary brain-washing in front of one screen or another, has killed family conversation and given the world a generation of scruffy, monosyllabic, crabby yobs, so has declined the wish to go anywhere and interact.

What people need is adventure, varied interactions and bracing fresh air!

Having undergone various fundamental conversions (such as giving up smoking), James Bond is, of course, still going strong. Then there are the really modern tales from *Mission Impossible* and *Jurassic Park*. They are all grist to the mill.

Even stories about animals, from Beatrix Potter's *Peter Rabbit*, to Kenneth Grahame's *Wind in The Willows* and Richard Adams' *Watership Down* have strong adventure themes.

Real Adventurers

Real adventurers are of a noble calling; they both hate and love secrets and the unknown. They are hunters, seekers and explorers who travel to inquire, probe, survey, uncover, define, catalogue, perpend and to understand.

Adventurers might be defining boundaries between nations, hunting tree or plant specimens, following river courses, following struggles, hunting wild animals, seeking out shrines and artefacts (or even lost cities and treasure), and then they give their knowledge to the world.

Maybe surprisingly, there are still vast wildernesses which are largely unknown. There are certainly depths of the ocean to which man has not yet plunged – and all the while man is exploring space.

Beyond any doubt, the 'civilised' (or should I just say increasingly 'urbanised') human race is becoming far too chair bound and content to take 'celluloid', second-hand adventure from the television and computer screens. There is even some sad-minded, 'Lara Croft'-style computer 'game', modelled on the two real missions performed by Violette Szabo GC, an agent for the SOE in the Second World War (recounted in this book). Given that Violette was caught, mercilessly tortured and interrogated and, refusing to assist her captors with one iota of information, shot at the age of twenty-three with her corpse hurriedly burned in a concentration camp crematorium, one wonders what kind of people come up with the idea to make a computer game out of her hopelessly glamourized life; a game for lazy slob-children to play in darkened rooms on summer holiday in sunny seaside towns with the waves crashing a hundred yards away. One also wonders what is wrong with the lazy slob-children themselves and then, also, what is wrong with their parents – but then I suppose that it is obvious that they must be lazy slobs too.

Thoughtlessness, insensitivity and naked commercialism are big bugbears of our age and they find willing victims, especially in the impressionable young. Creativity and the spirit of adventure in the young need to be encouraged more if the European nations are to find their way out of the social and economic mess they are in. It is a great pity that many schools substituted teaching computer technology for teaching wood and metalwork, but thank goodness for such organisations as the Duke of Edinburgh's Award Scheme and Operation Raleigh (the idea of modern adventurer Colonel John Blashford-Snell).

One very important thing I have learned from researching for this book, is that so-called 'New Woman' was around long, long before the Suffragettes of a hundred years ago and the 'Flower Power' militants of the 1960s, and, moreover, She was far more self-contained, independent and interesting than the generation of women who 'burned their bras' in mock protest at being 'female eunuchs'.

Long live real adventure and real adventurers!

Chapter 1

Lady Hester Lucy Stanhope (1776–1839)

> She left the web, she left the loom;
> She made three paces thro' the room,
> She saw the water-lily bloom,
> She saw the helmet and the plume,
> She look'd down to Camelot.
> Out flew the web and floated wide;
> The mirror crack'd from side to side;
> "The curse is come upon me," cried
> The Lady of Shalott.
> From *The Lady of Shalott* by Alfred, Lord Tennyson

LADY HESTER Lucy Stanhope was born on 12 March 1776 at Chevening, Kent. She was the eldest daughter of Charles Stanhope, Lord Mahon, heir to the Earl of Stanhope, and his first wife, Lady Hester Pitt, daughter of William Pitt The Elder (The First Earl of Chatham) and sister of William Pitt The Younger.

Hester's mother died when Hester was four years old and her father married again. Hester was an independent and determined child and she grew up to become a commanding and magnificent woman.

She remained at Chevening until 1800, when she went to live with her grandmother. In 1803 Hester went to live with Pitt The Younger at Walmer Castle, Kent, where she helped to create the gardens. She moved with Pitt to London when he became Prime Minister in his second Ministry from 1804.

At this time, Hester was exposed to the top end of the social spectrum and was at the very hub of political power. She was devoted to the bachelor Pitt and helped him by acting as his hostess. Hester was attractive, lively and good company, but she always had a tendency to speak her mind which offended some people.

Unfortunately, Pitt The Younger died in January 1806 – probably from complications arising from a consistent surfeit of port wine taken upon the advice of his doctors for his digestive problems. His personal debts of some forty thousand pounds were paid by vote of Parliament, which also gave Hester a pension of a miserable twelve hundred pounds a year.

Now Hester was outside the tent peering in; a person of no current importance. She found her position difficult and took it out on those around her.

In 1809 she suffered another setback in her personal life when both General Sir John Moore (to whom she had grown attached), and her half-brother were killed in the Napoleonic Battle of Corunna on 16 January.

Hester decided to sail first to Gibraltar and then to Malta to get away from it all. In Malta she met Michael Bruce, the son of a well-to-do businessman who was engaged in a tour. They fell in love and started living together.

The happy couple stayed in Malta for a while and then travelled to Constantinople. They were shipwrecked off the isle of Rhodes and eventually ended up in Cairo where they were received with honour by Mehmet Ali Pasha. They later took a tour of the Holy Land and the Lebanon. Hester was extravagant in her lifestyle and behaved as she wished.

Warned that when she entered 'fanatical', Islamic, Damascus she must behave as a local woman and veil herself, to the astonishment of observers, she instead dressed in male Turkish clothes and rode into town on horseback.

Hester stayed in Damascus for three months, attracting awe, rather than deprecation, and then decided she would be the first European woman to visit Palmyra ('The Bride of The Desert'), an ancient and ruined Syrian city, dating from the second millennium BC.

On 17 March 1813, dressed as a Bedouin male, she rode into Palmyra at the head of a caravan of twenty-two camels and a small army of Bedouin Arabs to be greeted warmly by the Emir. She always claimed that they and the inhabitants of the adjacent, modern town, crowned her *Queen of the Desert* under a triumphal arch!

Hester now decided the time had come for Michael to return to England and his family. She was to stay in Syria. So, the affair over, she dumped him and he left for good on 7 October 1813.

Just after this, Hester probably caught the Plague, which was rife at the time, and she was nursed by her own doctor and later biographer

(Dr Meryon), whom she had brought from England. Once recovered, but now without money from Michael Bruce's family and just her small pension to sustain 'The Queen of The Desert' Hester was taken to the sometime convent of Mar Elias on the mountains behind Sidon in the Lebanon. After that, she lived for a while at Deir Mashmousheh.

In 1815 Hester persuaded the Ottoman government authorities to join her search for buried treasure at Ashkelon, a port north of Gaza, based on the directions of a medieval, Italian document she had obtained. The treasure was supposed to be buried in the remains of a mosque in the port. The Governor of Jaffa accompanied her, but all they found was a large, headless statue which, in a fury, Hester ordered to be smashed up and cast into the sea. However, this probably does count as the first archaeological 'dig' with documentary references in the Holy Land.

In 1816 Hester waged a vendetta against a group of villages to avenge the death of a friend who had been murdered in the vicinity. She found herself short of money as a result of these excursions and had to borrow more and more. After living some years at Mar Elias and Deir Mashmousheh, she moved to Dar Djoun, a remote spot higher in the hills – indeed, on its own strategic hill with a true, panoramic view. Here Hester repaired an old building, (called 'Dahr El Sitt'), added others, laid out gardens, and fortified it all with a wall and gates. She lived here for the remainder of her life with a large (but gradually dwindling) household of servants, slaves and guards.

During the miniature civil wars for which the Lebanon is noted, and especially during the siege of Acre by Ibrahim Pasha of Egypt between 1831 to 1832, Hester gave sanctuary to numerous refugees – among them Druze, deserters and enemies of Ibrahim Pasha – and Emir Bashir Shihab II of the Lebanon (with both of whom she had previously been on good terms).

Despite threats and attempted persecution, she refused to surrender her authority or the men under her protection, guarded her fortress retreat and defied the world. Indeed, her local influence (borne out of strength of personality, rather than military might), was such that she did, more or less, rule the district around her.

Hester's health deteriorated rapidly as she grew older. There were physical and psychological symptoms, and she started flying into rages which were followed by depression and melancholy. She gave up on contact with the outside world and bemoaned her fate to the few left with her inside her walls. Curious visitors would be treated at night to endless talk of the old days and of her occult and mystic beliefs.

Despite the fact that she was no longer living in luxury, Hester continued to borrow money until a main creditor asked Mehmet Ali Pasha to help him recover what was owed.

Mehmet Ali approached not Hester, but the British Consul-General, who sent the matter to England. The Foreign Secretary, Lord Palmerston, decided that Hester's pension would have to be stopped in return for settlement of the debt.

She was given the decision by a letter dated 10 January 1838 and reacted with a last great flurry of angry correspondence. In August that year she arranged for publication of these letters in the newspapers but alas, it was to no avail.

Many of Hester's servants had already left for want of pay, some taking her goods as 'compensation', and the rest she dismissed. She completely retired from the world.

Her days of magnificence long behind her, Hester, 'Queen of the Desert', became a complete recluse and died alone and in squalor, on 23 June 1839 at Dar Djoun, where she was buried. However, she was restless even in death because her remains were reinterred in the British Ambassador's garden in Beirut on 2 February 1989. But even that was not the end of it because her ashes were finally scattered, amidst the ruins at Dar Djoun, on the anniversary of her birth, 23 June 2004.

Now, presumably, they will leave Lady Hester alone.

Chapter 2

Sir James Brooke KCB, DCL (Oxon), White Rajah of Sarawak (1803–1868)

Who is it that can tell me who I am?
King Lear 1.4.132, by William Shakespeare

T HERE HAVE been Englishmen sought out by foreign lands to rule them – apparently on the basis that an English gentleman with a sufficient fortune can meet any case. Harold Harmsworth, the first Lord Rothermere, was offered (and declined), the throne of Hungary in 1927 as a result of his support for a revision of the Treaty of Trianon in Hungary's favour. Academic, writer, publisher, diplomat and all-round sportsman, C. B. Fry claimed he had been offered the throne of Albania while attending the League of Nations in Geneva in 1920 but declined because he did not have a sufficient income to take it up. Apparently, Fry had a dry sense of humour and whether the offer was ever really made has never been substantiated by any official source. However, one man and the dynasty that followed him became, for a century, the absolute rulers of Sarawak, now one of two Malaysian states, on the northwest side of the island of Borneo. This original White Rajah even inspired Joseph Conrad's novel *Lord Jim*.

James Brooke was born on 29 April 1803 at Secrore, Benares, India. His father was a judge in a court of the East India Company and James spent the first twelve years of his life with his parents in India. Then he was sent to England to stay with relatives in Reigate, Surrey. They put him to board at Norwich Grammar School which he detested, running away, with impunity. When his parents returned from India and went to live in Bath, Brooke joined them. Apparently receiving little further formal education, in 1819, aged sixteen, he too, entered the service of the East India Company as an ensign in the Bengal Native Infantry. Brooke was eventually promoted to Sub-Assistant Commissary-General in 1822. He was very seriously wounded when commanding a troop of irregular cavalry in the course of the First Anglo-Burmese War in January 1825. He was awarded a pension for his injuries and returned to England to recover over the course of the next five years. Although he tried, Brooke found he was unable to return to service in India before the expiry of his leave and resigned his commission with the East India Company. He visited various countries including China, Malacca and Singapore, before again returning to England.

Brooke then unsuccessfully tried a trading trip to China and decided his father's suggestion that he was not cut out for trade was right. However, his father died in 1835 and left him the considerable fortune of £30,000. From this, and with his wilful nature and spoiled background, he bought a lightly-armed schooner which he named *The Royalist*. He recruited a crew and from late 1836 went on training missions around the Mediterranean Sea before setting sail for Singapore on 16 December 1838. He seems, at this time, to have had no set plan as to a particular endeavour, except to secure adventure. He certainly found it.

In Singapore, Brooke came across some British sailors who had been shipwrecked and had received assistance from Rajah Muda Hassim of Sarawak, the uncle of the Sultan of Brunei. The Governor-General of Singapore asked Brooke to go to Sarawak and thank the Rajah for his help. Maybe urged on by some thought of a main chance after learning that the Sultan of Brunei had been subject to a rebellion by disaffected Bidayuh antimony (mineral) miners on the island, Brooke accepted the commission. After sailing up the Sarawak River and anchoring at the capital, Kuching, he was received by the Rajah in August 1839. He learned about the nature of the rebellion from the Rajah and went on a fact-finding mission in the region, meeting local people, including Malays and Dayaks. At this stage, Brooke had evidently not found quite what he was looking for and he returned to Singapore.

However, in August 1840, he went back to Kuching where the rebellion was still raging. In return for a promise from the Rajah that, if he quelled the rebellion, the Rajah would secure his appointment as Governor of Sarawak, Brooke agreed to act.

Mustering his crew and the Rajah's forces, Brooke routed the rebels from their headquarters on the Sarawak River. However, the Rajah was not fast in realising his end of the bargain and Brooke was forced to use the threat of force to assist his memory. On 24 September 1841, Brooke trained his ship's guns on the Rajah's palace. The Rajah then conceded and Sultan Omar Ali of Brunei confirmed Brooke's appointment in July 1842. In

August that year, and in the face of open opposition from the old regime, he was created (officially) the First White Rajah of Sarawak at Kuching. Rajah Hassim returned to Brunei where Brooke's influence, backed-up with the threat of assistance from the Royal Navy, had him created the Sultan's Chief Minister in October 1843.

Brooke was now effectively an absolute monarch of an oriental kingdom and he appointed a London agent, Henry Wise, to secure official recognition by Britain and to promote his financial interests. However, Wise had his own ideas, and in 1848 he purported to grant an unauthorised mining concession in Sarawak. For the time being, The White Rajah and Mr Wise parted company.

The ideals behind Brooke's reign were those of a somewhat romantic orientalist: reform, stabilisation, modernisation, and an increase in free trade (avoiding the intercession of middlemen and mere profiteers), without disturbing local customs and traditions – except in the case of practices such as headhunting, piracy, and slavery, which offended his modern, humanitarian values and were gradually discouraged and then stamped out. Had he thought about it (and he probably did not), he might have seen himself as a kind of Platonic Guardian of the people in his charge. One thing is for certain, he would never have asked himself the question: '*Quis custodiet custodes ipsos?*' ('Who guards the Guardians themselves?')

Accordingly, Malay was kept as the official language, and although Brooke was a Christian (who would later encourage Christian Missions in Sarawak for the sake of stabilising his regime), he decreed that Islam was to be respected as a religion. He also imported Brunei law which he overlaid with notions of English equity and fairness. Brooke recruited men from the British army to assist him in his government. He was fortunate in inspiring a loyal following, but he also relied on the native hereditary aristocracy to tow the line and help him to guide the people forward.

Brooke almost certainly regarded his policies as philanthropic. He lightly taxed the native population but heavily taxed commercial production of things such as opium and arrack (a distilled alcoholic drink) which was largely in the hands of the Chinese. Brooke also set about putting down coastal raiding parties perpetrated by alliances between certain Dayak tribes and Brunei tax collectors (of all people), and he secured the support of the Royal Navy to do so. In mid-1843 and mid-1844, Brooke and a Captain Keppel RN, attacked the longhouses of the Dayak pirates.

Brooke even took one of his chief opponents, former Governor, Pengiran Ali, prisoner. These activities all resulted in a territorial expansion of Brooke's kingdom beyond the bounds of 'Sarawak Proper', and were recognised in a Treaty with the Sultan of Brunei in 1853. At Brooke's behest, Admiral Cochrane RN, destroyed the pirate base at Marudu in August 1845. This further hit coastal raiding, but in early 1846 the Sultan of Brunei ordered the killing of allies of Brooke and Hassim in Brunei. Enlisting Cochrane's help once again, Brooke secured the ceding to Britain, from the Sultan, of the island of Labuan.

In October 1847 Brooke returned to England where he found himself fêted as a self-motivated hero of empire and the celebrity of the moment. He was received by Victoria and Albert and honours were showered upon him (including an honorary DCL from Oxford University). He was made a Knight Companion of the Order of the Bath as well as being painted by Sir Francis Grant RA. Besides all this, Brooke was appointed Governor of Labuan and Consul-General for Borneo. He rested his own claims to legitimacy as Rajah on the agreement of senior Malay Chiefs, rather than on any Treaty with the Sultan of Brunei, and established an advisory council with Malay and European members, on which he was assisted by such as his private secretary (and later, biographer), Spenser St John.

Brooke was sensible enough to know that to reinforce his reforms – especially in relation to headhunting and piracy, as well as to educate the people – there should be the introduction of Christian Missions. He appealed to Oxford and Cambridge Universities and to the great Missionary Societies (the Society for the Propagation of the Gospel in Foreign Parts and the Church Missionary Society), for help, but none of them had the funds at the time to meet his requests. Accordingly, he established a new association, supported by his friends, called the 'Borneo Church Mission'. This association sent out some missionaries, the first of whom was the Rev F. T. McDougall, who was later consecrated the first Bishop of Labuan and Sarawak in 1855.

When McDougall arrived at Kuching in 1848, the Rajah gave him a large piece of ground on which to build himself a house, church and school. That same year, John Brooke Johnson, Brooke's elder nephew and heir apparent, also arrived to receive training in governing Sarawak. He changed his surname to Brooke and became Brooke Brooke. He had a son called Hope Brooke. James Brooke's younger nephew, Charles Brooke, arrived in Sarawak in 1852 to assist his uncle in administration.

Brooke was anxious that the Dayaks, who lived out of town and had their home in the jungle, should also be taught. By this time, and after all his experiences, Brooke was keen to spread the Christian word. Accordingly, he sent for more assistance from England and a second wave of missionaries arrived to live and work among the Dayaks in the jungle.

The Borneo Church Mission ran down for lack of support, and in 1854 the Society for the Propagation of the Gospel in Foreign Parts stepped in and took up the work.

Captain Arthur Farquhar RN was engaged to take action against the rebellious Dayaks of Saritas. The result was the Battle of Beting Marau on 31 July 1849 when many of these Dayaks were killed. Brooke then set about building forts to control traffic on the major rivers.

Meanwhile, in 1850, Brooke, as Governor of Labuan, was sent by the British Government to negotiate over trade with the King of Siam. However, he was largely ignored on his arrival and utterly failed in his mission. To make matters worse, Cochrane and Farquhar claimed large prize money through the naval court in Singapore which resulted in controversy in the press and criticism of Brooke's rule by radicals. There was even a commission of inquiry in 1854 with Brooke's thwarted former London agent Henry Wise dishing the dirt.

Eventually, Brooke was cleared of misfeasance but he had been shattered by the experience. A dose of smallpox and consequential scarring, added to his ills and he fell into a decline.

In 1857 (coincidentally the year of the Indian Mutiny) with Brooke no longer enjoying the support of the Royal Navy, four thousand Chinese gold miners revolted and invaded Kuching with a view to revolution. The Borneo Company and Charles Brooke, with loyal Dayak troops, just saved the day, but Brooke lost his house and personal possessions and counted himself lucky to have escaped with his life.

The Borneo Company was the only public company allowed to trade in Sarawak, and after the rebellion Brooke borrowed £5,000 from it to repair the damage. But the company soon wanted repayment, leaving Brooke's friend Baroness Burdett-Coutts to bail him out. The result of all this was that Brooke suffered a debilitating stroke in England in 1858.

Hard-pressed, he offered Sarawak for sale to recover his losses and then dropped a real bombshell. He acknowledged one Reuben George Walker (a stable-hand) as his illegitimate son and took him to Sarawak. This alienated the heir apparent, Brooke Brooke, who ended up disagreeing with his uncle so spectacularly that he and his son (Hope Brooke) were eventually disinherited in 1863.

In 1862 before he finally left Sarawak, Brooke officially acquired areas of Muka and Oya from the Sultan of Brunei, as well as another area on the Dutch border which had been taken by force by his nephews three years before.

On 25 September 1863 the First White Rajah of Sarawak left his realm for the last time, leaving Charles in charge. At last, the British Government recognised the State of Sarawak and its White Rajah, but Baroness Burdett-Coutts (who had repaid the loan to the Borneo Company), more or less owned it, so Brooke named her as his heir. However, she later renounced her rights, freeing Brooke to name Charles.

Brooke returned to England, more or less destitute and lived in seclusion in a house called Burrator, in the village of Sheepstor, on Dartmoor, south Devon, (a million miles from Sarawak), which was bought by public subscription. Brooke never reconciled with his elder nephew Brooke Brooke or Brooke Brooke's son Hope Brooke, and there were some who regarded Charles as treacherous in ousting them from the succession. However, James Brooke did make provision for the illegitimate son, whom he acknowledged, and for an illegitimate half-brother.

In 1866, Brooke suffered another stroke but lived on until a third carried him off on 11 June 1868. With all his adventures behind him, he was buried in Sheepstor churchyard. A monument to him was erected in Kuching. Charles, austere and parsimonious, succeeded him as White Rajah, continuing the same policies of beneficent (but now diluted) autocracy, until his own death in 1917 when the title passed to the third and last White Rajah, playboy Charles Vyner de Windt Brooke, whose half-hearted and erratic rule finally ended when Sarawak became a Crown Colony in 1946. Charles Vyner, the last White Rajah, died in a flat in Paddington, London, in 1963.

Now all three White Rajahs of Sarawak, with their century of autocratic, oriental rule, lie at rest together inside a railed enclosure in Sheepstor churchyard, on Dartmoor. Maybe, that is the unlikeliest part of it all.

Chapter 3

Richard Lemon Lander (1804–1834)

'Though we have adverted to the fact but seldom, nevertheless, throughout nearly the whole of our painful journey, we were both indisposed in a greater or less degree. In short, a very few days only had elapsed after our landing at Badágry, when we began to feel the debilitating effects of the African climate, and to experience a degree of languor which not even the warmest enthusiasm could wholly overcome. It is almost unnecessary to add that our spirits often sank under the depressing influence of this powerful adversary, whose inroads on our constitutions we had no means of resisting.'

From Richard and John Lander's *Address to The Public*

RICHARD LEMON Lander was born in the Fighting Cocks Inn (later renamed The Dolphin) in Truro, Cornwall, on 8 February 1804. His father, John, was the landlord. His mother had been born Mary Penrose. Probably inspired by the tales of travel and adventure told by sailors and others in his father's inn, Lander seems to have been unusually adventurous from the first. He walked to London at the age of nine to find excitement and in 1815, aged eleven, went to the West Indies as a passenger's servant on a merchant ship, not returning until 1818. He grew into a short, slight youth with light-coloured hair. He was again employed by a ship's passenger and went to the Cape of Good Hope between 1823 and 1824. By the age of twenty-one Lander had seen a good part of the then known world.

In 1825 he joined the expedition of Captain Hugh Clapperton RN, initially as little more than a servant, to explore the River Niger. At an early stage of this expedition all the other European members of the team died. Clapperton himself died at Sokoto in 1827, and Lander, as the sole European survivor, had to walk for seven months, retracing his steps back to the coast. Even so, he was not out of it that easily. The King of Badágry accused him of witchcraft and forced him to drink poison, much as the British used to try alleged witches by dunking them in water. Lander survived and the Africans very reasonably concluded that he was not a witch after all and let him return to England in July 1828. He published *The Journal of Richard Lander from Kano to the Sea Coast* as well as *Records of Captain Clapperton's Last Expedition to Africa and The Subsequent Adventures of The Author*.

Lander then took a job in the Truro Customs House and married Ann Hughes, the daughter of a London merchant and had a surviving daughter, Harriett Ann. However, wanderlust was now in his blood and a letter from the Admiralty to the Colonial Office in 1829 suggested Lander as an appropriate choice to conduct further exploration of the Niger.

The truth is that the small amount of money that they could get away with paying him impressed them as much as anything and his appointment was confirmed for the expedition in 1830, under terms of reference of ascertaining the course of 'The Great River' and its termination. They even allowed him to take his younger brother John with him on the basis that he would not be paid at all! The purpose of taking John along was that because he had stayed at school until the age of fifteen, he was better able to keep a journal.

The expedition left on 9 January 1830, bearing many gifts to pacify local tribes. These included 110 mirrors, 100 combs, 50,000 needles, 100 tobacco pipes, 38lb of beads, 100 snuff boxes, 64 arm bands, 50 yards of red cloth and two bugles! It arrived on 22 February 1830.

On the way, the men stopped at Cape Coast Castle (now part of Ghana) to recruit a Hausa guide, called Pascoe, whom Lander had used on his former expedition. Their plan was to follow Clapperton's route overland to Badágry.

The King of Badágry was busy executing a large number of local people and let the Lander party pass after they had paid him a tribute of sixty-two ounces of gold.

The party then trekked five hundred miles over four months, and ended up being held to ransom for five weeks by the Sultan of Yauri before he let them go. Once they got away, they entered the river near Bussa – where Scottish explorer Mungo Park (1771–1806) had drowned twenty-four years earlier. They then descended the river in canoes (towards the Gulf of Guinea), exploring as they went. In the town of Rabba it was plain that the people had never seen white men before and they recorded:

'The people stand gazing at us with visible emotions of amazement and terror; we are regarded, in fact, in just the same light as the fiercest tigers in England.'

They started down the river on 2 August and encountered – and survived – various dangers, including crocodiles, hippopotami and a whirlpool. Then, on 25 October, they were sitting on the riverbank when armed tribesmen rushed at them. Instead of defending themselves, they decided to stand up, disarm themselves and hold their hands out peaceably. The tribesmen stopped. Their chief later explained he had thought they were his enemies from across the river but when he saw their white faces and that they were unarmed, he had believed that they were 'Children of Heaven, dropped from the skies.'

Continuing on the descent of the river on 5 November, Lander's team saw fifty war canoes coming towards them. The canoes were armed with cannons and the men carried muskets. Despite the fact that they flew, amongst others, a Union flag, they turned out to be river pirates and robbed the Landers, leaving them with virtually nothing. The men feared they would be finished off, but the pirates instead took them on a three-day journey to Kirree (now Asaba), where they sold them into slavery to King Obie of the Eboes. This strange man was decked out in necklaces of coral and broken looking-glass, worn so tight as to cause his neck and face to appear inflamed. He also wore short trousers and bells around his ankles.

The Landers's interpreter tried to talk them out of their predicament, but after two days the King decreed that they should be sold to King Boy of Brass Town. The brothers were appalled at their situation; not least because nearly everywhere they had been they had been treated with respect, even veneration, and now they found themselves categorized as 'the most degraded and despicable of mankind.'

After three days in King Boy's canoe, they noticed the surge of tidal water around the boat. They then passed through mangrove swamps of the Nun distributary and towards the Gulf of Guinea. The King knew there was a British ship moored offshore and intended to leave John Lander as a hostage and take his brother to the ship's Captain to demand a ransom for their release. It turned out that four of the crew were dead and four others too sick to work. The Captain nearly refused to help but eventually pretended to agree to pay a ransom because he saw that the Lander brothers could at least help him to get the ship under weigh. Eventually, John arrived at the ship and the ransom was evaded. The ship got away in a tempest, but a sandbar looked so perilous that wreckers and pirates sat around waiting to scavenge the wreck.

The Landers disembarked at Fernando Po (now Bioko) and took another ship home after it had taken its regular voyage to Rio de Janeiro. They arrived in Portsmouth in June 1831.

The journals for which John had been principally responsible were published by John Murray and made them quite a bit of money. *A Journal of The Expedition to Explore the Course and Termination of The Niger* proved that the Niger flowed through many mouths into the Gulf of Guinea as well as revealing the river's source and route.

The Landers were then received by King William IV. In 1832 Richard was made the very first recipient of the RGS's Gold Medal for having proved that the Niger and the Nile were different rivers.

However, the Colonial Office still refused to give John anything and even refused a small pension for Richard.

After this, Lander took a job in the Liverpool Customs House where he attracted the attention of a local Scottish businessman, Macgregor Laird, who determined that the Niger was a place worth exploring for the purposes of trade. He set up an expedition, including a supply brig and two of the first ocean-going steamers

The expedition set off for West Africa on 25 July 1832 to investigate commercial opportunities of the Niger and arrived, after many delays, on 7 October. Lander left the steamers and entered the Nun distributary, proceeding upstream. The party was fired on at Angiama by hostile African trading middlemen along the river who wished to restrict foreign traders to the coast. Richard Lander was hit – rather unsportingly – in the backside, and fell mortally wounded.

The musket ball had lodged too deep in his thigh for surgery and the wound turned gangrenous. He died on Fernando Po on 6 February 1834. He is buried and commemorated there. Friendly Africans called him 'Nasarah Curramaee', meaning 'Little Christian'. Macgregor Laird and R. A. K. Oldfield published an account of *An Expedition into the Interior of Africa* in 1835. The failure of the expedition quelled immediate enthusiasm for further ones.

Lander had named an island in the River Niger 'Truro' and called a hill on its banks 'Cornwall Mountain'.

There is a rudely-executed replacement statue of Richard Lander on a tall column at the top of Lemon Street in Truro (the original had been executed by Neville Northey Burnard but fell shortly after it was erected). In 2004, the 200th anniversary of Lander's birth, Steve Dunstone, FRGS, led an expedition, including two of Lander's descendants, in his footsteps down the Niger.

There is a joint commemorative plaque to Mungo Park and Richard Lander on the banks of the 2,600–mile River Niger: '*…. who traced the course of the Niger from near its source to the sea. Both died in Africa for Africa*.'

John Lander (1807–1839) also died young from a disease that he had probably contracted in Africa.

The discovery of the Niger delta was not just an interesting discovery in itself, but also opened up the possibility of trade with West Africa, starting with palm oil which had many uses from making soap to machinery lubricant, and was, consequently, much in demand. The trading posts also enabled missionaries to go and, backed by the Royal Navy, to force the end of African slavery – by that, I mean slavery amongst the Africans. In these days of popular revisionist history, it is often wrongly assumed that white Europeans (and white Americans) are the only slave-masters ever to have existed. In fact, black Africans had been in the trade from time immemorial and, like the Greeks and the Romans too, felt that slavery was the natural lot of conquered people (Britons had been enslaved by the Romans). Moreover, the slave-traders of Europe would have been hard-pressed to have engaged in their hideous trade had it not been for the active co-operation of black African slave masters. Indeed, in the course of their adventures, described above, we know that Richard and John Lander had themselves been rendered into slavery there.

Richard Lander would have been glad of this important by-blow of his great efforts. As he once said: 'Slavery is by far the most appalling evil that can befall the human race.'

Besides the plaque on the River Niger and the statue in Truro, Richard Lander's name is also commemorated in a school and museum in modern Nigeria.

Chapter 4

Mary Seacole (ca. 1805–1881)

'Gently comes the world to those
That are cast in gentle mould.'
Editor of Mary Seacole's autobiography

MARY JANE Seacole (née Grant) was born in Kingston, Jamaica, to a Scottish soldier and a Creole owner of a military boarding house, in around 1805. Her mother had nursing skills as well as knowledge of Creole medical treatments and herbals and, in childhood, Mary soon started practising the cures on dogs and cats. Later, after yearning to visit England – 'I never followed with my gaze the stately ships homeward bound without longing to be in them' – Mary then had the opportunity to travel to London twice in the 1820s with relatives. The second time she took Jamaican pickles and preserves to sell. On the return journey, the ship caught fire and they all nearly perished. Back in Kingston, she married Edward Horatio Seacole (a godson of Admiral Lord Nelson's) on 10 November 1836. They established a store on the Black River on Jamaica's south coast, but Edward was in delicate health and, despite Mary's best efforts, they had to return home where he died a month later. Mary's beloved mother also soon died and she was left alone. Mary continued to provide nursing care and run the boarding house; even rebuilding it after the Kingston fire of 1843. Having made the decision to resist further offers of marriage, she also continued making and selling preserves to make ends meet. In 1850 there was a great cholera epidemic in Jamaica (maybe brought ashore with dirty laundry from a ship) and she nursed victims during this time. In the same year Mary decided to go to help her brother in Panama, where he ran a hotel and a store, and set about making great provision for the journey with food and clothing.

In her autobiography, Mary details the dreadful journey to Cruces, including the river trip up the Chagres River, with ague and fever raging all around. At long last, her brother met her on the rickety wharf and conducted her to his Independent Hotel, which turned out to be a log cabin full of Californian gold miners. However, once she was fed, as she says, 'I soon forgot my troubles in the novelty of my position.'

Shortly after, there was an outbreak of cholera. It began with an old friend of her brother's whom he had just fed. He fell very ill and died in convulsions of pain. There was suspicion of poisoning, but Mary viewed the corpse and from her recent experiences of cholera in Jamaica, knew the cause. But none immediately thanked her for her advice. Then she saved a second victim and became sought after for her advice, but the local people did not make any efforts to clean up their houses and the filthy streets. Mary was soon working flat out and once even found herself preferred over a Spanish doctor who arrived to help. A one-year-old child died in her arms and she decided to perform an autopsy on it to help her in the battle against the disease. She tended a local grandee's wife and child but they both died. Mary returned to her brother realising that the cholera had come upon her, its greatest foe.

Fortunately, it was a mild attack and abated by the next day, but still left Mary exhausted. Within a few weeks the outbreak itself began to subside but Mary still had several patients. Soon she decided to take on a hut opposite her brother's place and turn it into a small restaurant, offering dinners at four shillings each.

Eventually, though, after a brief stay down river and having reconciled herself to the fact that her brother would not return to Jamaica, she decided to return alone. She bought a passage aboard an American ship but found herself unwelcome as a 'nigger' and 'yaller woman' amongst the fine American ladies in the saloon. After remonstrance, she was refunded her passage money and took a British ship instead.

Mary landed in Jamaica and remained there for eight months, during which time an outbreak of yellow fever raged.

She then returned to Panama to wind up her business there. What would become the Crimean. War had already between declared between Russia and Britain, France and Turkey and she was determined to go to England and then to the war zone to help nurse the sick and wounded.

In the autumn of 1854 Mary landed in England and set about trying to involve herself in the nursing War Effort, in which Florence Nightingale was a pioneer. The battles of Balaclava and Inkerman, and the storm of 14 November, had proved the existing hospital services of Scutari inadequate. It was, she said, her 'judicious decisiveness' that spurred her on.

First she tried the War Office but advanced nowhere; having even beset the house of the Secretary at War's private address. She was told by a member of the Nightingale administration that the nursing service (such as it was) was 'full' and that there were no vacancies. She disbelieved the woman who told her this and suspected that she was not wanted owing to the colour of her skin. Eventually, at the end of her tether, Mary stood in the street, looked up at the grey London sky and, to the astonishment of onlookers, prayed aloud for guidance and for help. Her mind cleared overnight and the next day she resolved to go to the Crimea under her own steam. She even announced her intention, to open a hotel and soldiers' mess, on printed cards which she sent on ahead. Then she met a relative of her late husband, a Mr Day, (who was going to the Crimea on shipping business), and they agreed together to open the hotel and a store. Mary then stocked up (at her own expense), with medicines and 'home comforts', and took a ship called the *Hollander*, bound for Turkey.

Before she eventually left Constantinople, she took a small ship to Scutari in order to see the hospital and to meet Florence Nightingale, and this is what happened:

'*I am admitted to Miss Nightingale's presence. A slight figure, in the nurses' dress; with a pale, gentle, and withal firm face, resting lightly in the palm of one white hand, while the other supports the elbow – a position which gives to her countenance a keen inquiring expression, which is rather marked. Standing thus in repose, and yet keenly observant – the greatest sign of impatience at any time a slight, perhaps unwitting motion of the firmly planted right foot – was Florence Nightingale – that Englishwoman whose name shall never die, but sound like music on the lips of British men until the hour of doom.*

She has read Dr. F—'s letter, which lies on the table by her side, and asks, in her gentle but eminently practical and business-like way, "What do you want, Mrs. Seacole – anything that we can do for you? If it lies in my power, I shall be very happy."

So I tell her of my dread of the night journey by caique, and the improbability of my finding the "Hollander" in the dark; and, with some diffidence, threw myself upon the hospitality of Scutari, offering to nurse the sick for the night. Now unfortunately, for many reasons, room even for one in Scutari Hospital was at that time no easy matter to find; but at last a bed was discovered to be unoccupied at the hospital washerwomen's quarter.'

In the morning Mary returned to the *Hollander*. In the reference to Miss Nightingale's impatient foot and between the lines of Mary's eulogy to her, we may, perhaps, detect Mary's acceptance of a final, polite, official rebuff.

Mary then sailed across the Black Sea to Balaclava. Her husband's relative, Mr Day, arrived to greet her and she transferred to the *Medora*, announcing her arrival to her acquaintances. She was met by such as Sir John Campbell, the CO of a Division. Mary then had more trouble in trying to stall the sailing of a ship on which some of her supplies were stored and she spent most of her time with the supplies under a tarpaulin on the wharf. She started assisting the grateful doctors with the wounded as soon as she could, as well as making cakes and lemonade for them, and was surprised one day when the hard-faced Admiral whom she had convinced to reluctantly stall the sailing of her supply ship came up to her, clapped her on the shoulder and said with some emotion, 'I am glad to see you here, old lady, among these poor fellows.' Sometimes, the men that she came across she had known from their visits to Kingston, and they greeted her warmly.

Mary slept over casks of gunpowder and cases of cartridges on board the *Medora*, and there was a need to keep a watchful eye against plunder of stores and enemy incendiaries.

Eventually, Mary and Mr Day established their store, Spring Hill, near Balaclava, although a flood carried away some of the provisions and nearly drowned her. When the summer was nearly over, the British Hotel was nearly finished too, but it was never entirely completed. The magazine *Punch* later published a verse or two including:

> 'The cold without gave a zest no doubt,
>   To the welcome warmth within;
>   But her smile, good old soul, lent heat to the coal,
>   And power to the pannikin.'

Mary had spent £800 on the building, but she also suffered great losses through theft of the supplies. However, it must be stated that her purpose with the store was selling provisions and foods such as chicken broth, roast fowl, and so on. Nevertheless, her book contains many great testimonials to her services overall, including a quotation from the great *Times* war correspondent W. H. Russell.

On page 187 in the 2nd volume of Russell's *Letters from the Seat of War*, is the following entry:

'In the hour of their illness these men (Army Works Corps), in common with many others, have found a kind and successful physician. Close to the railway, half-way between the Col de Balaclava and Kadikoi, Mrs. Seacole, formerly of Kingston and of several other parts of the world, such as Panama and Chagres, has pitched her abode – an iron storehouse with wooden sheds and outlying tributaries – and here she doctors and cures all manner of men with extraordinary success. She is always in attendance near the battle-field to aid the wounded, and has earned many a poor fellow's blessings.'

Mary describes a typical day in the Crimea for her:

'They were all pretty much alike, except when there was fighting upon a large scale going on, and duty called me to the field. I was generally up and busy by daybreak, sometimes earlier, for in the summer my bed had no attractions strong enough to bind me to it after four. There was plenty to do before the work of the day began. There was the poultry to pluck and prepare for cooking, which had been killed on the previous night; the joints to be cut up and got ready for the same purpose; the medicines to be mixed; the store to be swept and cleaned. Of very great importance, with all these things to see after, were the few hours of quiet before the road became alive with travellers. By seven o'clock the morning coffee would be ready, hot and refreshing, and eagerly sought for by the officers of the Army Works Corps engaged upon making the great high-road to the front, and the Commissariat and Land Transport men carrying stores from Balaclava to the heights. There was always a great demand for coffee by those who knew its refreshing and strengthening qualities, milk I could not give them (I kept it in tins for special use); but they had it hot and strong, with plenty of sugar and a slice of butter, which I recommend as a capital substitute for milk. From that time until nine, officers on duty in the neighbourhood, or passing by, would look in for breakfast, and about half-past nine my sick patients began to show themselves. In the following hour they came thickly, and sometimes it was past twelve before I had got through this duty. They came with every variety of suffering and disease; the cases I most disliked were the frostbitten fingers and feet in the winter. That over, there was the hospital to visit across the way, which was sometimes overcrowded with patients. I was a good deal there, and as often as possible would take over books and papers, which I used to borrow for that purpose from my friends and the officers I knew. Once, a great packet of tracts was sent to me from Plymouth anonymously, and these I distributed in the same manner. By this time the* *day's news had come from the front, and perhaps among the casualties overnight there would be someone wounded or sick, who would be glad to see me ride up with the comforts he stood most in need of; and during the day, if any accident occurred in the neighbourhood or on the road near the British Hotel, the men generally brought the sufferer there, whence, if the hurt was serious, he would be transferred to the hospital of the Land Transport opposite. I used not always to stand upon too much ceremony when I heard of sick or wounded officers in the front. Sometimes their friends would ask me to go to them, though very often I waited for no hint, but took the chance of meeting with a kind reception. I used to think of their relatives at home, who would have given so much to possess my privilege; and more than one officer have I startled by appearing before him, and telling him abruptly that he must have a mother, wife, or sister at home whom he missed, and that he must therefore be glad of some woman to take their place.*

Until evening the store would be filled with customers wanting stores, dinners, and luncheons; loungers and idlers seeking conversation and amusement; and at eight o'clock the curtain descended on that day's labour, and I could sit down and eat at leisure.'

In the third week in June the third bombardment of Sebastopol began with the regiments mustering and marching overnight of the 17–18 June. Early in the morning, Mary took her supplies with a team and, getting through a road block by force of character and reputation, went to Cathcart's Hill. From there, and frequently under fire, she nursed the sick and ministered to their needs of supplies, before returning to Spring Hill in the evening. On 19 June there was an Armistice and she returned to the battlefield, where, besides the wounded, cholera had broken out. Mary notes with sadness the death of Lord Raglan, whom she had known and who had shown a great concern for his injured men. She goes on to relate the terrible battle of Tchernaya on 16 August, at which she mentions that she nursed and ministered to Russian as well as British troops; even rescuing from being 'put down' an orphaned and wounded Cossack colt, which she eventually took back to England with her.

Mary was there for the fall of Sebastopol in September and even attended the ceremony during the final moments when the Orders of the Companions of the Bath were handed out to those who had earned them. She received a pass to enter the ruined city but, because of the mischief of a boy, was briefly arrested as a spy, before being released and returning to Spring Hill.

Eventually, formal peace came early in the New Year and the last salvos fired were to salute it.

Mary describes the leave taking of the Crimea as follows:

'We were among the last to leave the Crimea. Before going I borrowed a horse, easy enough now, and rode up the old well-known road – how unfamiliar in its loneliness and quiet – to Cathcart's Hill. I wished once more to impress the scene upon my mind. It was a beautifully clear evening, and we could see miles away across the darkening sea. I spent some time there with my companions, pointing out to each other the sites of scenes we all remembered so well. There were the trenches, already becoming indistinguishable, out of which, on the 8th of September, we had seen the storming parties tumble in confused and scattered bodies, before they ran up the broken height of the Redan. There the Malakhoff, into which we had also seen the luckier French pour in one unbroken stream; below lay the crumbling city and the quiet harbour, with scarce a ripple on its surface, while around stretched away the deserted huts for miles. It was with something like regret that we said to one another that the play was fairly over, that peace had rung the curtain down, and that we, humble actors in some of its most stirring scenes, must seek engagements elsewhere.

I lingered behind, and stooping down, once more gathered little tufts of grass, and some simple blossoms from above the graves of some who in life had been very kind to me, and I left behind, in exchange, a few tears which were sincere.

A few days later, and I stood on board a crowded steamer, taking my last look of the shores of the Crimea.'

Mary ends her book (which sold very well), with a list of those who chose to help her upon her eventual bankruptcy back in England; a bankruptcy caused by having been forced to use her own private means to accomplish her goal of helping and nursing the sick and those injured in the cause of a country which in so many ways had been officially reluctant to recognise her worth. The names of early subscribers to her cause were:

> Major-General Lord Rokeby, K.C.B.
> H.S.H. Prince Edward of Saxe Weimar, C.B.
> His Grace the Duke of Wellington.
> His Grace the Duke of Newcastle.
> The Right Hon. Lord Ward.

General Sir John Burgoyne, K.C.B.
Major-General Sir Richard Airey, K.C.B.
Rear-Admiral Sir Stephen Lushington, K.C.B.
Colonel M'Murdo, C.B.
Colonel Chapman, C.B.
Lieutenant-Colonel Ridley, C.B.
Major the Hon. F. Keane.
W. H. Russell, Esq. (*Times* Correspondent).
W. T. Doyne, Esq

She was also supported by *The Times* and *Punch* magazine, and eventually, the Queen approved a 'Seacole Fund', under Royal Patronage, to ensure that she was reimbursed her losses and taken care of. Mary died suddenly at her home in London on 14 August 1881. She is buried in Kensal Green Roman Catholic cemetery, beneath a monument which reflects her many achievements in alleviating human suffering wherever she found it: in Kingston, Panama and in the Crimea.

All the world commemorates Florence Nightingale, 'The Lady With The Lamp', as a pioneer of modern nursing on the edge of battle, but Mary Seacole has a claim to be commemorated as one of the first modern women routinely to chance dangers over extended periods, in areas of high contagion and, dodging shells and bullets, to take aid and assistance to wounded men (regardless of their allegiance), on the very battlefield itself.

Chapter 5

Jane Elizabeth Digby (1807–1881)

'...Some woman's yellow hair
Has maddened every mother's son.'
From *September 1913* by W. B. Yeats.

THERE MUST be something in the idea of the strength of bloodlines as Jane Digby's great-great niece, The Hon Pamela Churchill Harriman (1920–1997), daughter of Lord Digby, successively wife of Randolph Churchill, Layland Hayward, and Averill Harriman, and also US Ambassador to Paris, was often described as 'the twentieth century's greatest courtesan'. Jane Digby (often erroneously called 'Lady' Jane Digby), could certainly have laid claim to the same title for her own century, and even stood out amidst the much stiffer competition of the Restoration age.

Jane, sometimes nicknamed 'Aurora', was born on 3 April 1807, at Forston House on the estate of her father, Captain (eventually Admiral) Sir Henry Digby and his beautiful wife Jane Elizabeth (née Coke). Jane's father had enriched the family with the prize from his capture of a Spanish ship, and had been one of Nelson's Captains at the Battle of Trafalgar.

Jane was a lovely-looking child with a wonderful face framed in golden hair, big, wide-set, blue eyes, and growing tall with a perfect figure. She became accomplished as a painter, sculptress and musician, as well as learning nine languages.

In 1824, at the age of seventeen, she was married (as his second wife), by arrangement, to Lord Ellenborough, who was twice her age and destined to become Governor-General of India and Lord Privy Seal (the keeper of the Sovereign's personal seal). Jane seems at first to have settled down into the life of a socialite but then fell in love with a librarian, called

Frederick Madden. However, instead of pursuing this interest, she went to London and began an affair with her cousin George Anson, which caused comment in her circle but no open scandal. On 15 February 1828, she bore her husband a son, Arthur, who died shortly afterwards.

It was at this point that Jane's real career really began. She met Prince Felix Ludwig Johann von Nepomuk Friedrich zu Schwarzenberg, the Austrian attaché in London, and became his mistress. This time there *was* an open scandal and Lord Ellenborough probably fought the Prince in a duel. He received a substantial sum in damages. In 1829 Jane left Ellenborough for good and went to Basel where, on 12 November 1829, she gave birth to Schwarzenberg's daughter, named Mathilde Selden. This child was later taken in and brought up by Schwarzenberg's sister in Switzerland. Jane moved to Paris in 1830 and openly lived with Schwarzenberg which, according to the official morality of the age, limited her social opportunities. However, by now, Ellenborough had had quite enough and, for the sake of his honour and his family name, he went to the lengths of obtaining the passing of a Private Act of Parliament, by which he divorced her.

Jane bore Schwarzenberg a second child, Felix, in December 1830 but he soon died. Not long after this, Schwarzenberg, with an eye to his career and appeasing his family, left her. She took her daughter to Munich, where she met and became friendly with Ludwig I of Bavaria and possibly became his mistress, as well as the mistress of Baron Karl Theodore Herbert von Venningen Üllner, probably by whom she bore a son, Filippo Antonio Herberto, on 27 January 1833 in Palermo. In the summer of that year she left her son and went to Germany. Still apparently hoping for reconciliation with Schwarzenberg, Jane nevertheless, married Venningen Üllner in November.

Had her career of bolting and affairs ended at this point, it would have been remarkable enough, but she had far to go and, by the end, would have made the notorious Georgiana, Duchess of Devonshire, of the preceding generation, look like Little Bo Peep.

In August 1834 Jane bore Venningen Üllner a daughter (Berthe). Later that summer she met Honore de Balzac, who undoubtedly used her as a template in his writings. She made a visit to Munich in 1835 and there met a Greek called Count Spiridion Theotoky. Her affair with him was discovered by her husband and he wounded Theotoky in a duel but then, rather sportingly, let him recuperate in Schloss Venningen. In the Spring of 1839 Jane left her family to go to Paris with Theotoky and bore him a son (Leonidas) on 21 March 1840. This child seems to have been the only one she much cared for. Her husband agreed to give her a divorce on good terms but she had the marriage annulled by the Greek Orthodox Church (incidentally bastardizing Berthe).

Maybe it is a testament to male vanity that each of the men through whom she ran at such a pace must have considered himself up to retaining her when so many others had failed. Jane married Theotoky in Marseilles in 1841 and seemed then to settle down at his estate at Dukades in Corfu.

In about 1844 she probably had an affair with King Otto of Greece, son of Ludwig I, which seems to have gone unchallenged, but then tragedy struck when her beloved son Leonidas, aged six, fell off a balcony and was killed in front of her very eyes. The allocation of blame for this incident provoked a separation from Theotoky, and in 1852 Jane fell in with a sometime Albanian brigand-turned-Greek-Court member called Cristos Hadji-Petros whom she followed to his mountain lair, as his consort, living a wild bandit existence, in hidden caves and riding furious horses. Her marriage to Theotoky was annulled (once again this was done by the Greek Orthodox Church) but, discovering that her brigand had been unfaithful, she did not (as had been her intention), marry him. Instead, now aged forty-six, alone again and still seeking adventure, she travelled east. Jane landed in Syria in May 1853 and promptly fell in love with her host, a Bedouin called Saleh, before travelling to Damascus where she fell in with the Mesreb tribe and met Abdul Medjuel al-Mesreb who later became their leader.

After an absence abroad, Jane returned to Syria in November 1853 to discover that her latest beau, Saleh, had married someone else. On the rebound, she embarked on a torrid and ill-fated affair with Sheikh al-Barrak during 1854.

Meanwhile, Medjuel had divorced his wife and Jane finally set her cap at him, capturing him in a Muslim marriage in 1854, against his family's wishes. In fact, it might be noted in passing, that according to Islam, a Muslim man may marry a non-Muslim woman who can keep her own religion because she is not going to change her husband's religion. But a Muslim woman may not marry a non-Muslim man because he might well persuade (or compel) her to abandon Islam. In any event, Jane kept her religion but she did learn Arabic and adopted eastern dress and customs. She split her time between a house in Damascus, where she developed a library and kept an English garden and horses, and the rest of her time she spent in desert sojourns with her husband – with whom she was a party to the kidnapping and holding to ransom of hapless tourists.

In 1859 she rendered help to Christians in Damascus who were attacked by the Druze and when peace was restored she began to receive European travellers.

When posted in 1869 to the Consulate at Damascus, Sir Richard Burton made friends with Algerian hero and exile Abd el Kadir who was a kindly man, always dressed in pure white and carrying jewelled arms. Lady Burton, on the other hand, befriended the notorious Jane Digby el Mezrab. Sir Richard mistrusted her from the first, presumably believing, in his half-enlightened way, that sexual and romantic adventure were reserved to the male of the species.

From Thomas Wright's *Life of Sir Richard Burton*, we learn of Jane at this time (leaving the spellings as found there):

> 'Says Mrs. Burton of her new friend, "She was a most beautiful woman, though sixty-one, tall, commanding, and queen-like. She was grande dame jusqu'au bout des doights, as much as if she had just left the salons of London and Paris, refined in manner, nor did she ever utter a word you could wish unsaid. She spoke nine languages perfectly, and could read and write in them. She lived half the year in Damascus and half with her husband in his Bedawin tents, she like any other Bedawin woman, but honoured and respected as the queen of her tribe, wearing one blue garment, her beautiful hair in two long plaits down to the ground, milking the camels, serving her husband, preparing his food, sitting on the floor and washing his feet, giving him his coffee; and while he ate she stood and waited on him: and glorying in it. She looked splendid in Oriental dress. She was my most intimate friend, and she dictated to me the whole of her biography." Both ladies were inveterate smokers, and they, Burton, and Abd el Kadir spent many evenings on the terrace of the house with their narghilehs. Burton and his wife never forgot these delightsome causeries. Swiftly, indeed, flew the happy hours when they "Nighted and dayed in Damascus town.........."'

Burton had scarcely got settled in Damascus before he expressed his intention of visiting the historic Tadmor in the desert. It was an eight-day journey, and the position of the two wells on the way was kept a secret by Jane Digby's tribe, who levied blackmail on all visitors to the famous ruins. The charge was the monstrous one of £250, but Burton—at all times a sworn foe to cupidity—resolved to go without paying. Says Mrs Burton: 'Jane Digby was in a very anxious state when she heard this announcement, as she knew it was a death blow to a great source of revenue to the tribe… She did all she could to dissuade us, she wept over our loss, and she told us that we should never come back.' Finally, the subtle lady dried her crocodile tears and offered her 'dear friends' the escort of one of her Bedawin, that they might steer clear of the raiders and be conducted more quickly to water, 'if it existed'. Burton motioned to his wife to accept the escort, and Jane left the house with ill-concealed satisfaction. The Bedawi in due time arrived, but not before he had been secretly instructed by Jane to lead the Burtons into ambush whence they could be pounced upon by the tribe and kept prisoners till ransomed. That, however, was no more than Burton had anticipated. Consequently, as soon as the expedition was well on the road he deprived the Bedawi of his mare and accoutrements and retained both as hostages until Damascus should be reached again. Appropriately enough this occurred on April the First. Success rewarded his acuteness, for naturally the wells were found, and the travellers having watered their camels, finished the journey with comfort.

The party reached Damascus again after an absence of about a month. The Bedawi's mare was returned and Jane had the pleasure of re-union with her *dear* Mrs Burton, whom she kissed effusively.

Jane Digby did finally settle down and remained with her Sheikh through many desert nights.

After such a life one might almost expect Jane to have been struck by a bolt of lightning or to have been the object of a hail of arrows or stones from angry wives, but no. She died (rather unromantically), of dysentery, on 11 August 1881, and was buried in the Protestant cemetery in Damascus.

Chapter 6

General Sir James Abbott KCB (1807–1896)

And wilt thou return, when the bright dreams of morning
Are fading before the sad Herald of Day?
From a poem by James Abbott, written at Mhow, 1 March 1832

THERE IS great irony in the fact that Osama bin Laden was brought to book in Abbottabad, a military town in the Himalayan foothills of North West Pakistan. It is still named, long after British imperial withdrawal, after James Abbott, who had devoted a part of his life to quelling religious extremism and pacifying the surrounding district of Hazara, which came into his charge, as its administrator and then First Deputy Commissioner, between 1849 and 1853.

Abbott was born on 12 March 1807, the son of a retired Calcutta merchant, of Blackheath, then a village in Kent. It was a remarkable family. Abbott was the brother of Major-General Augustus Abbott CB, an Indian Army officer (with whom he served); Major-General Sir Frederick Abbott CB; Major-General Saunders Alexius Abbott, an officer in the East India Company army, and Keith Edward Abbott, a Consul General in the diplomatic service. Abbott was educated at a school in Eliot Place, Blackheath, where a fellow pupil was future Prime Minister and favourite of Queen Victoria, Benjamin Disraeli, who was instrumental in creating Victoria Empress of India in 1877.

Abbott later received military training at the East India Company's military training centre, Addiscombe College, near Croydon, and was commissioned into the Bengal Artillery as a second Lieutenant in June 1823.

He arrived in India in December 1823 but his first experience of action did not come until the second siege of Bharatpur, between December 1825 and 18 January 1826 in the First Sikh War. He was under the command of his brother Augustus when the fortress was stormed and taken. In 1827 he was promoted to Lieutenant and made adjutant of the Sirhind division of artillery. In these years Abbott saw little action, but between October 1835 and August 1836 he was assigned to the revenue survey of Gorakpur and was transferred to the survey of Bareilly, receiving official commendations for his efforts. This all resulted in his promotion to brevet Captain (a temporary rank) in June 1838.

In November of that year, he was part of the army of the Indus under Sir John Keane which was under the excuse of supporting a pro-British puppet ruler, Shuja Shah Durrani, according to the declarations in the Simla Manifesto of 1838. The British feared the increasing influence of Russians and Persians in Afghanistan – a gateway to India and far from the support of British naval forces. Afghanistan was the centre of what came to be called the 'Great Game' involving tensions between, and secret exercises by, both sides. The disastrous First Afghan War was the result and it dragged on until 1842, resulting in British withdrawal and military humiliation.

In April 1839 Abbott reached Kandahar and was then sent as a political officer to Herat. Meanwhile, Russia had sent a military expedition to Turkestan, against the Khanate of Kiva, ostensibly seeking the release of Russian slaves there but, in reality, seeking to expand Russian influence in the region. The ruler of Kiva, Allah Quli Khan, was initially refused military backing by the British, but in December 1839 Abbott was sent on a mission to Khiva to attempt to persuade the Khan to release Russian slaves and so deny the Russians an excuse for war. If war had already broken out, Abbott was told to try to mediate a settlement.

As it had turned out, the Russian expedition had turned back because of adverse weather conditions. However, the situation was not actually resolved and Abbott recorded that he felt handicapped by ignorance of the place, its people, language and customs. Nevertheless, he managed to advise that British military aid should be sent to aid the Khan, but despite later claims, he did not persuade the Khan to free the Russian slaves. He went on, though, to agree to provide a British agent at Khiva and to conduct mediation between Khiva and Russia. He even set out in March 1840 to travel to Russia to make a start. This was all beyond his authority and on his own initiative and resulted in his caravan being taken hostage by Khazakhs in April 1840. Abbott was severely wounded in the right hand in a skirmish but the Khazakhs, fearing retribution, released him and his party. Eventually, they arrived in St Petersburg where the attempt at mediation failed. However, for such a brave attempt under threatening conditions, he was later thanked by the British Foreign Secretary, Lord Palmerston, promoted to the substantive rank of Captain and given a pension for his injuries.

The Russian slaves in Khiva were later freed; not as a direct result of Abbott's own efforts but those of his successor. Nevertheless, he claimed the credit for ending Russia's excuse to intervene in the region and wrote his own account of his efforts in the published journal mentioned below.

In 1841 Abbott returned from Britain to India where he first held a post in the Merwara local battalion before being transferred in 1842 to be assistant to the Resident of Indore. A marriage in 1844 produced a daughter but sadly ended in his wife's death in 1845 shortly after which came his most famous appointment, as First Deputy Commissioner of Hazara. It was during Abbott's time as one of Brigadier-General Sir Henry Lawrence's 'Young Men' deployed in advising the Sikhs after the First Sikh War (ending in 1846) that Lawrence described Abbott as 'of the stuff of the true knight errant'. Lawrence was the founder of the Lawrence Schools which are still prestigious academic institutions, and he died defending Lucknow during the Indian Mutiny in 1857.

As part of the Treaty of Lahore, following the end of the First Sikh War in 1846, Hazara and Kashmir were transferred to Raja Gulab Singh. Gulab Singh lost control of Hazara and exchanged it for Jammu. Consequently, the British appointed Sardar Chatar Singh as Nazim (regional administrator) and Abbott as his assistant to quell unrest in the region and to undertake a survey of the revenues. Abbott succeeded in all this by learning the language, culture and religion of the people, and in promoting their social and economic interest – even with a vastly inferior force holding the Marquella Pass against the Sikhs until the Second Sikh War ended in February 1849. He received the thanks of the Governor-General and of both Houses of Parliament.

Abbott was promoted brevet major in June 1849. As a result of the annexation by the East India Company of the Punjab after the end of this War, he was appointed First Deputy Commissioner. Between 1852 and 1853, for the sake of strategy and climate, he moved the seat of Government from Haripur to a site higher up, which became the town of Abbottabad but, much against his personal wishes, he was transferred away, in early 1853, before the town (which is his memorial), was properly established.

Before he left Abbottabad, Abbott wrote an Ode to the place (which, for all its sentiment, is not amongst his best poetry), and threw a party which lasted (after the fashion of certain Asian celebrations), for three days and three nights; his final departure being attended by 'a large and lamenting crowd of people'.

Abbott was promoted to Lieutenant-Colonel in 1857 and finally attained the rank of General on his retirement in 1877. He had married again in 1868, but, having borne a son, that wife also died within a short time of their marriage. Abbott was made a Companion of the Order of the Bath in 1873 and advanced to a Knight of that Order in 1894.

In his Journal *Narrative of A Journey from Heraut to Khiva, Moscow and St Petersburgh* Abbott wrote of his experiences on that journey. These included an unusual eulogy on a pilau with young camel flesh which he was served under a blue sky after a long period of privation, and of having to make do with sour curds, sweetened with snow water. He summed up his harsh experiences as follows:

'In the brief space recorded in these volumes the author lived many years (if reckoned by suffering, thought, anxiety, experience) of ordinary human existence. He had the advantage of viewing events and feelings generally widely scattered, condensed together into a closeness of contact that admitted of the strongest contrasts, and most searching comparisons. The one great object of his search through life, he kept constantly before his eyes: endeavouring to divest his mind of prejudice and partiality, and by rigid analysis, to separate the most pure gold of truth, from every debasing alloy.....It pleased Heaven, by a tissue of remarkable and unexpected events, to carry him through all his adventures, and to crown his efforts with the most signal success.'

Of the particular journey and its objectives (both staving off Russian ambition in Afghanistan and the North West Frontier and the freeing of Russian slaves in Khiva), Abbott's conclusion of 'a most signal success' for himself is, as already remarked, wide of the mark. However, his overall achievement in bringing peace and prosperity to the region of Hazara which he governed at least as much for the well-being of its people as for the good of the Empire which he served, it is most surely right.

Abbott retired to Ryde on the Isle of Wight, where he lived quietly; dying on 6 October 1896. He is buried with his second wife in a cemetery in Guildford, Surrey.

Chapter 7

Colonel John Whitehead Peard, 'Garibaldi's Englishman' (1811–1880)

'A man who has not been in Italy, is always conscious of inferiority, from his not having seen what it is expected a man should see.'

Dr Samuel Johnson

JOHN WHITEHEAD Peard was born in Fowey, Cornwall, in July 1811, second son to Vice-Admiral Shulham Peard and Matilda (née Fortescue, of Penwarne). He attended King's School, Ottery St Mary, Devon, and went up to Exeter College, Oxford, from which he emerged with an MA. He was a man of gigantic stature and enormous strength, and later, when he had his beard, he could easily have been mistaken for Giuseppe Garibaldi himself. It was said that Peard had the 'shoulders of a bull', and was the stroke of the college boat as well as the terror of the town roughs. In 1837 he was called to the Bar by Inner Temple and on a Grand Day there, is supposed to have drained a loving cup of up to two quarts of wine.

He seems to have practised at the Bar on the Western Circuit for some time and married Catherine Augusta Richards, the daughter of a former headmaster of Blundell's School in Tiverton, Devon. Tiring of the Western Circuit, Peard became a Captain in the Duke of Cornwall's Rangers between 1853–1861.

The movement for Italian Unification ('Il Risorgimento') was a social and political movement to bring together the different states of the Italian peninsula. It might be said to have begun in 1815 at the Congress of Vienna after the Battle of Waterloo, and the end of Napoleonic rule across much of Europe, and to have ended completely with the Franco-Prussian War of 1870–1871. However, Colonel Peard, Garibaldi's Englishman, was not actively concerned in very much of it. There were two prominent radical Italian figures in the movement. One was Giuseppe Mazzini, a political figure, and the other was Giuseppe Garibaldi, born in Nice and a citizen of the kingdom of Sardinia. After taking part in a failed uprising in Piedmont in 1834, he had fled to South America and only returned to Italy in 1848, where he still interested himself in Italian unification.

On his visits to Italy, Peard was annoyed at the arrogance and brutality of Neapolitan officials and in 1860, he volunteered to join Garibaldi's forces, enlisting in the Cacciatori delle Alpi Volunteer Corps. He followed Garibaldi in his Sicilian campaign, where he showed notable courage at the battle of Milazzo in 1860 and was promoted to Colonel. Peard was also there in Garibaldi's victorious advance on Naples and was made commander of the English Legion. However, despite his own personal 'gallantry and indifference to danger', Peard was not a great commander and his regiment was eventually disbanded. However, even though there was still far to go in the Italian unification movement, the Neapolitan campaign had resulted in the proclamation on 17 March 1861, of Victor Emmanuel as King of a united Italy, and Peard was at Villino Trollope in Florence during the celebrations of Italian liberation on 2 June 1861.

King Victor Emmanuel awarded Peard the Cross of the Order of Valour and, out of gratitude, Garibaldi later built him a house back in his native Cornwall.

In 1864 Garibaldi visited England and spent 25–27 April at Peard's original house, 'Penquite', near Fowey.

The West Briton of 29 April 1864 reported Garibaldi's visit to England: 'He travelled to Plymouth by train, where he was given a rapturous welcome. Everybody made a great fuss of him. There he stood in his red shirt and grey trousers, with pale face and his dark beard… still protesting against hero-worship.

Soon after nine o'clock on Tuesday morning, the domain of Penquite became the focus of attraction to persons anxious to see Garibaldi. They came flocking toward it from all directions and in all sorts of vehicles not only the villages immediately contiguous, but some of the adjoining towns contributed larger numbers of their inhabitants…'

A little girl called Polly was handed up for his blessing and W. B. Rands then wrote a poem called *The Girl That Garibaldi Kissed*, which includes the verses:

'He bowed to my own daughter,
And Polly is her name;
She wore a shirt of slaughter,
Of Garibaldi flame, –

Of course I mean of scarlet,
But the girl he kissed – who knows? –
May be named Serena Charlotte
And dressed in yellow clothes.'

Actually, the world did learn the exact identity of that little girl. Sir Arthur Quiller-Couch tells us in his charming collection of essays *From a Cornish Window*, that he knows her name because he eventually married her! Her name was, in fact, Louisa Amelia Hicks.

Later, as mentioned above, Garibaldi commissioned an Italian architect to build a villa for Peard on the Little Pinnock estate, off the main Fowey to St Austell road. The imposing result, 'Trenython', dating from 1872, is still there. After Peard left, it became a residence of the Bishop of Truro and then a convalescent home for railway men. Now (predictably), it is a country club and holiday resort, although well preserved. There is an ancient Celtic cross in the gardens. A red cloak that had belonged to Garibaldi may be seen in Fowey Museum, Trafalgar Square, Fowey.

Peard died on 21 November 1880, at Trenython, and was buried in Fowey cemetery.

Chapter 8

John William Colenso, 1st Anglican Bishop of Natal (1814–1883)

'It is our bounden duty 'to buy the truth' at any cost,
  even at the sacrifice, if need be, of much,
  which we have hitherto held to be most dear and precious.'

John William Colenso

T HE TOWN of St Austell in Cornwall was for a long time, a prosperous, and somehow also, picturesque Cornish mining town; first for tin and copper and then China clay. It is set on the sides of wooded valleys through which flows the combined River Vinnick and the Gover Stream. It was in St Austell, on 14 January 1814, that John William Colenso was born to John William Colenso (senior), a successful mining agent and his wife, who both happened to be enthusiastic members of the Congregational Church; although they switched to the Church of England when John William was in his teens.

The family initially lived in some style at Pondhu, on the immediate outskirts of the town and the boy was educated in the classics and mathematics in a local school. But his mother died when he was fifteen and a mine in which his father had an interest, was flooded by the sea, straitening the family's financial circumstances. They moved to a smaller house in Elm Terrace where, A. L. Rowse tells us, well into the twentieth century, a window pane bore his scratched initials 'JWC'.

In any event, there was no money to continue Colenso's schooling and he went to work as an usher at a school in Dartmouth. However, he seems to have managed to coach himself well enough in mathematics to enter St John's College, Cambridge, as a sizar in 1832. A sizar at Cambridge was a student admitted free of payment for tuition, but not, as sometimes suggested, in return for the performance of menial tasks for other students. Colenso was able to earn money from teaching and supported himself towards his degree, which he took in 1836, as Second Wrangler (that is with the second-best first-class honours degree), and as Smith's Prizeman. He was duly elected a fellow of the College.

Colenso was then appointed mathematics tutor at Harrow School in 1838 and ordained in 1839, and he also ran a boarding house for pupils but, instead of producing additional income, it caught fire and he lost all his possessions and fell into a large debt. Seeking to mend his fortunes, he returned to his fellowship at St John's College and wrote two books: one on mathematics and one on algebra. These books soon became (and, for long, remained), staples of the curriculum in schools up and down the country and Colenso profited from them to such an extent that he was in a position to marry and settle down. On 8 January 1846, he married Sarah Frances Bunyon of a Highgate family, whose head was involved in commerce in the city. Her family secured Colenso a country living as a priest of Forncett St Mary in Norfolk, where he carried on tutoring mathematics as well as editing a religious journal.

Puritanical though his early upbringing had been, Colenso had already begun to question the doctrine of everlasting damnation and punishment as consistent with an all-loving God and the teachings of Christ. However, it was more his interest in overseas missions that reached the notice of Robert Gray, the then Bishop of Cape Town, whose See (jurisdiction of a Bishop), was being divided, and Colenso was offered, and then accepted, the See of Natal in April 1853 and went there after his consecration in November. He spent ten weeks touring and later published a paper on his findings. The point was to raise money and find missionaries to carry out the work, but he was increasingly crossing the line of orthodoxy even at this early stage and went so far as advocating that polygamy (including that of the Zulus who were to be the main beneficiaries of Anglican Christian conversion) was not inconsistent with the Christian tradition. Colenso eventually set out his thinking in a paper called *The Proper Treatment of Polygamy*. One can imagine how this went down in certain orthodox Christian quarters of that age. However, although he would have preferred his converts to be monogamous, the thrust of his point was that it was far better to be a Christian polygamist than not a Christian at all. Moreover, if monogamy was a condition precedent to conversion to Christianity, this would have a destructive effect on family life, cause any extra wives to be disowned, and the status of their children would be questioned.

It was in May 1855 that Colenso arrived with his family and mission staff to take up their duties. He decided from the first that his mission was to be aimed at the indigenous people. He even went so far as to live outside the main colonial townships and made his home at Bishopstowe, six miles outside Pietermaritzburg, which was also his chief mission station, called Ekukhanyeni ('The Place of Light'). Of course, this choice of location hardly endeared him with the white colonists. He even went so far as to try to enforce strict adherence to the Book of Common Prayer which, even then, some were trying to amend.

Within two years Colenso had built the Cathedral at Pietermaritzburg as well as churches in Durban and Richmond. Four mission stations in Natal and Zululand followed. He learned Zulu to teach, prepare and confirm, before going on to publish a Zulu grammar and Zulu-English dictionary, and to translate large parts of the Bible and the Book of Common Prayer into Zulu.

However, he had his detractors, personified in James Green, the Dean of Pietermaritzburg, an advanced Tractarian (a follower of the 'Oxford Movement', founded in Oxford in 1833, whose members favoured a return to the early teachings of the Roman Catholic Church; they had published ninety 'tracts' or papers, explaining their views). The Dean and his followers accused Colenso of holding liberal opinions and the Dean's sympathisers went so far as to burn effigies of Colenso in public places. The world forgets, in the face of the very visible 'Islamic fundamentalists' of the modern age, how much harm and injury has been done in the world by equally miserable proponents using their own brands of 'fundamental Christianity' as their tool.

In 1859 Colenso made a journey to meet Mpande, King of the Zulus and his son Cetshawayo, (their king during the Zulu Wars). The result of this journey was a publication called *First Steps of the Zulu Mission*.

Colenso's wife was a well-educated and supportive woman, and a friend of Frederick Maurice, a Unitarian turned Anglican who sought to interpret the Bible.

I have spoken of Colenso's Zulu 'mission' and 'Christian conversion' but his real objective, as it evolved, was to introduce Christianity into the Zulu tradition and culture. However, besides the influence of Frederick Maurice and his own early doubts about the existence of eternal punishment, as Colenso taught the Zulus, so they questioned him about aspects of the Bible that seemed to be at variance with nature (this was an age in which natural science was a moving force), and also about the massacres and horrors perpetrated in the Old Testament as alleged emanations of God's will and purpose. Gradually, Colenso moved towards biblical criticism and in 1861 produced a publication on the Book of Romans, in which his central theme was that God's purpose was not to punish sin but to eradicate it. This really put the liberal cat amongst the Tractarian pigeons and he was accused of contravening the thirty-nine articles of the Church of England which, presumably, were said to hold that God inflicts eternal punishment on sinners and that they eternally burn in hell. His next critical work, in 1862, examined the Book of Joshua. It followed his reading of much German biblical criticism and he concluded (in a nutshell) that, if biblical statements were plainly untrue then there were no binding lessons to be drawn from them. With this line he upset even his wife's revisionist friend Frederick Maurice.

As A. L. Rowse has said in relation to the stained glass window depicting Christ before Caiaphas for trial and which commemorates Colenso in St Austell church, the Scripture chosen beneath it is 'obtuse':

'He hath spoken blasphemy'

Bishop Gray who had been created Metropolitan Bishop by letters patent when his See had been divided, involved Colenso in his plans for the overall development of the Church in South Africa, but after the critical essays referred to above, he decided to try Colenso for heresy. In December 1863 he purported to summon a metropolitan court which comprised himself and two other bishops as assessors. Colenso refused to appear – except by a proxy – to object to their jurisdiction. The Court declared that it was deposing Colenso on 16 December 1863. He refused to recognise the declaration and so they then purported to excommunicate him.

Colenso brought a Petition of Right against the Crown which proceeded before the Judicial Committee of the Privy Council, and in a judgment given on 20 March 1865, the proceedings of the metropolitan court were set aside for want of jurisdiction. The Privy Council went on to hold that the letters patent of both Gray and Colenso were invalid because both the Cape and Natal had their own legislatures but that, nevertheless, by them, the Crown had created ecclesiastical persons and that only the Crown could undo them. On the substantive charge of heresy, there was no argument or decision. Colenso had won a long and hard fight against bigotry and the procedural irregularities that are frequently devised to inflict it.

However, victory came at a price. First of all Gray and his supporters secured the passing of a local constitution which provided for the Church of the Province of South Africa which some said was inconsistent with the established Church of England. Nevertheless, a new Bishop was consecrated under it in Cape Town in 1869 without letters patent from the Crown. Many Bishops then tried to stop Colenso furthering his mission within their dioceses but others supported him and a point was made when the Dean of Westminster Abbey invited Colenso to preach there. Moreover, ironically, Colenso's high profile resulting from the litigation stirred up interest in the man and swelled his congregations.

There was even a further civil case, which came before Lord Romilly MR, called *The Bishop of Natal –v– Gladstone & Others* which was concerned with Colenso's diocesan income. The Colonial Bishopricks' Fund threatened to withhold the diocesan income from Colenso. However, the Court pronounced that he was entitled to all the property of the See. The colonial courts also supported him and adjudged him in possession of all the churches, land and property belonging to the Church of England. The new establishment had to start again; even to the extent of building a new Cathedral and Churches.

However, the private subscriptions of the missionary societies were withdrawn from Colenso, but to balance that out, the clergy of Britain subscribed to a testimonial to him which helped him to continue his work. From all of this we may deduce that besides a capacity for deep scholarship across a wide spectrum, from mathematics to scripture, one of Colenso's chief qualities was steadfastness in the face of opposition and adversity.

Colenso went on to champion the cause of Hlubi, the Chief of the Langalibalele, when he was accused of the crime of ignoring a summons to account for the fact that his tribesmen had failed to register certain firearms. He withdrew to Basutoland after a fight in which some colonial administrators had been killed but was captured and tried in a Court claiming to be under 'native custom' and with Lieutenant-Governor Pine presiding as the 'Supreme Chief'. The Court's procedure involved giving its verdict, hearing the evidence and then allowing the defendant to be represented! He was then sentenced to be transported to the Cape. Other tribes also suffered confiscations of land and property as a result of the case. Colenso denounced the proceedings and campaigned in England for intervention. Lord Carnaervon, the Colonial Secretary, recalled the Lieutenant-Governor and directed the imposition of lesser sentences, but Colenso's opponents had found even more reasons to revile him.

When the Zulu War erupted in 1879, Colenso sided with the Zulus, asserting that King Cetshawayo's actions when the British had invaded his lands had been wholly defensive and that British officials, including the

High Commissioner, Sir Bartle Frere, had misrepresented the situation and were the ones truly responsible for the consequential war. Colenso was accused of making inflammatory statements and of inciting rebellion, although it is probable that Colenso's eldest son had such a grip on the situation that, had the British allowed him to mediate between them and the Zulus, the bloody massacres that followed could have been averted.

However, as it was, the Colenso stand on the issue made him even more unpopular with white colonists. After the war he campaigned for Cetewayo in London (where the King was eventually exiled), and Queen Victoria received King Cetshwayo (she was rather disappointed that he came not in his Chief's robes but in a western-style suit).

Cetshwayo eventually returned to Zululand in 1883 and there was an attempt to restore him to at least part of his kingdom, but owing to disagreement amongst the Zulus themselves, it failed and he died on 8 February 1884; the last Zulu King of an independent kingdom. His son succeeded him but he ruled only with Boer support.

Meanwhile, despite the deep love and support of his family and his faith, but no doubt worn down by his tribulations, Colenso had died on 20 July 1883. Known to, and remembered by, the Zulus as Sobantu ('Father of the People'), he is buried in his own Cathedral:

'In manus tuas Domine'

His children, notably Francis (Frank), Harriette and Frances Ellen, continued his fight for the rights of the indigenous population, and if anyone would have immediately recognised the justice behind the later, twentieth-century fight against the vicious apartheid that had its roots in nineteenth-century, colonial South Africa, it would have been these whom A. L. Rowse rightly described as the 'Controversial Colensos'.

Chapter 9

Sir Richard Francis Burton KCMG, FRGS
(1821–1890)

'Do what thy manhood bids thee do, from none but self expect
  applause;
He noblest lives and noblest dies who makes and keeps his self-made
  laws.
All other Life is living Death, a world where none but Phantoms dwell,
A breath, a wind, a sound, a voice, a tinkling of the camel-bell.

From *The Kasîdah of Hâjî Abdû El-Yezdî; A Lay of the Higher Law*
(a pretended translation), by Richard Francis Burton

RICHARD FRANCIS Burton was probably one of the most original
and picturesque Englishmen of all time and was both a polyglot and
polymath of extraordinary accomplishment. Lord Derby said of him:
'Before middle age, he compressed into his life more of study, more of
hardship, and more of successful enterprise and adventure, than would
have sufficed to fill the existence of half a dozen ordinary men.'

Richard Francis was born on 19 March 1821 at Torquay, Devon, the eldest
son of Colonel Joseph Netterville Burton and Margaret Beckwith Baker.
Burton is a Romany name and Richard later claimed that he was descended
from Louis XIV, through one of his mistresses. Through his maternal
grandfather, Richard Baker, (Squire of Elstree, Hertfordshire) he was
certainly descended from the Scotch brigand, Rob Roy ('Red') MacGregor.
Baker was ecstatic when little Richard was born with flaming-red hair and
although it later turned black, his temper remained red to the end. As an
aside, Colonel Burton's brother, Francis, was a military surgeon who took a
death mask of Napoleon which became a centre of great controversy.

The Burtons were a Westmorland family who had settled in Ireland and
then washed up in Torquay. Not long after Richard was born, he and his
parents went to live with the Bakers in Elstree.

Suffering from asthma, Colonel Burton took his family abroad. Richard Burton's life of travel began almost immediately as, apart from a short spell in a school at Richmond, most of his early years were spent travelling between France, Italy and Elstree.

Mr Baker resolved to leave all of his considerable fortune to Richard, cutting out Richard's mother and a half-brother, but at the moment he stepped out of his carriage to attend his lawyer's office to remake his will, he dropped dead. The old will stood and Richard Burton would have to make his own way in the world.

Burton's father obviously could not have understood his son very well as he wished him to become a clergyman, and so up he went up to Trinity College, Oxford in 1840. His father refused to let him leave.

Markedly independent, rebellious, obstreperous and pugnacious throughout his life, in April 1842 Burton deliberately defied a College order that undergraduates must not attend the Oxford Races. He was not the only offender but, unlike the others, he refused to accept that the order had been reasonable in the first place and declined to apologise for breaking it. The others were merely rusticated but Burton was expelled and that was the end of his Oxford career and his father's hopes of a clergyman son. He lied to his family and said that he had been granted an extra vacation for academic excellence, for which his father then gave a dinner. But the truth came out and there was an ugly scene.

Despite the evident streak of rebelliousness, Burton then asked to be commissioned into the army. His father agreed and bought him a commission as ensign to the 18th Regiment of Bombay Native Infantry (of the East India Company). He left England on 18 June 1842.

In India he fell in with what were then usual British customs and soon had an irregular attachment to a Hindu woman (Bubu). It connected, he said, 'the white stranger with the country and its people, gave him an interest in their manners and customs, and taught him 'thoroughly well their language'. Such an arrangement was sometimes known as a 'sleeping dictionary'. It is notable that those Britons who served in the Empire in the early to mid-nineteenth century did not withdraw themselves from the local people whom they ruled as they did in the twentieth century when 'going native' was something that came to be avoided. Burton also took with him his bull terrier and kept a fighting cock.

In 1844 he was posted to Sind where his innate aptitude for learning languages blossomed still further.

Burton also took to roaming through local society disguised as a half-Arab/half-Persian character called Abdullah of Bushire (choosing a person of mixed race allowed him more easily to cover any mistakes that he might make in language or customs). General Sir Charles Napier who had annexed the province of Sind (announcing it in a telegram which read, as a pun, '*Peccavi*' – 'I have sinned' in Latin), made use of Burton's aptitudes and had him explore local society and bring him news, especially of unrest or impending trouble. During this time, by means of trading in bits and pieces, Burton acquired much local knowledge. Napier even had him do a written report on local male brothels for the purpose of suppressing them and as part of the exercise of bringing English law and order to bear. However, the very existence of the report seemed to have an adverse effect on Burton's military career and without the slightest reason at all, gossips started wondering how far Burton had taken his research! When he later applied for the post of chief interpreter for the force, and despite his high attainment in so many languages including even Sindi and Sanskrit, he was declined in favour of a man with English and just one other language.

Burton, at this time was aware of certain contradictions in his nature such as his love of animals but his propensity for cock-fighting, and his high ambition was hampered by his violent temper. He became ill and was given two years' leave. He went to Goa, then Panany and the Neilgherries. Now he was reading and translating the verse of Luiz Vaz de Camões ('the Portuguese Shakespeare'). Back in Sind, he became a student of Sufi-ism. His eyes had become too weak to return to surveying and that is when he applied for, and was refused, the post of interpreter. Failure to win the post had a devastating effect on his morale and sense of justice.

In 1849 Burton was given home leave on grounds of ill health, taking with him a mass of material on which he would later build his translation of *The Thousand Arabian Nights and One Night*. During his convalescence he travelled in Italy, and it was from Ariosto – or perhaps through Camões, who adopted it – that he took his life motto, 'Honour, not honours'—

> '*Tis honour, lovely lady, that calls me to the field,*
> *And not a painted eagle upon a painted shield.*'

Burton also wrote the first four of his many books; *Goa and the Blue Mountains* (1851), *Scinde, or, the Unhappy Valley* (1851), *Sindh, and the Races that Inhabit the Valley of the Indus* (1851) and *Falconry in the Valley of the Indus* (1852).

He met his future wife in Boulogne in 1851. One day he was strolling on the ramparts when he saw her and some other girls but, with her stature, blue eyes and her tumbling, auburn hair, she especially stood out. Her name was Isabel Arundell and she was of an old Roman Catholic family. Burton chalked on a wall, 'May I speak with you?' and left the piece of chalk there. She wrote back, 'No, mother will be angry', but said to herself, 'That is the man'. Eventually, they were formally introduced and could speak together. But they would not marry for another ten years.

It was around this time that he met Forster FitzGerald Arbuthnot who entered the Bombay Service in 1852 and quickly rose to be a 'Collector' (a district head of local administration). He influenced Burton in relation to the importance of translating oriental literature, seeing it as important as ancient Greek and Latin.

Burton, earned his *brevet de pointe* for the excellence of his swordsmanship, and became a Maitre d' Armes in Boulogne. As a swordsman, horseman and marksman, few were his equal in the army.

In 1852 Burton proposed to the RGS that he attend Hajj, the annual Muslim pilgrimage to Mecca and Medina which all Muslims are supposed to undertake at least once in their lives. Very few non-Muslims have infiltrated these events and lived to tell the tale and Burton was aware that discovery of his true identity could well have imperiled his life. He secured RGS support and finally set out in 1853, determined to adopt his usual oriental identity. He perfected the chanting of Muslim prayers and the costume, and hennaed his face and limbs. However, once in Cairo, on the advice of Haji Wali (who would become a lifelong friend), he changed his persona into that of an Afghan doctor. Burton kept the fast of Ramadan, donned the clothes of a pilgrim and also displayed a star sapphire. He arrived in Yambu, the port of Medina, on 17 July and joined a caravan for Medina where he visited various sites of interest including Mohammad's tomb.

Travelling then to Mecca, he worshipped at the Prophet's Mosque and saw the Kaaba. 'There at last it lay', cries Burton, 'the bourn of my long and weary pilgrimage, realising the plans and hopes of many and many a year.' The Kaaba is a large, curtained, rectangular structure and is the holy centrepoint of Muslims' prayers. They turn to face its bearings when they pray.

Burton made his seven anti-clockwise circuits of the Kaaba and eventually reached the sacred black stone, which he thought was probably aerolite (from a meteorite). He visited the Zem Zem well and prayed at the praying place of Abraham. The next day he went to Mount Arafat, where he was among fifty thousand, and on the third day, he stoned the pillar which represented the devil. He had his head shaved and his nails clipped. He even managed to go inside the Kaaba which he described as a simple place with a marble floor and hung with gold-flowered, red damask. It had a flat roof, three cross beams and three central columns. There were lamps of gold. In short, he had completed his pilgrimage.

Burton visited the tomb of Eve at Jeddah and then boarded an English ship and left off his disguise. His exploit immediately made his name for daring, which he wrote up in his *Pilgrimage to Al-Madinah and Meccah*. A rumour started that he had killed a man who had seen through his disguise and, enjoying shocking people, Burton let it run. He also started a history of Islam which he called *El Islam*, which was later published unfinished. Burton then travelled to Bombay, meeting James Grant Lumsden of the Bombay Council, on the way.

Staying with Lumsden in Bombay, he conceived the plan to go to the forbidden city of Harar and set off for Aden where he discussed plans for The Arabian Nights with his friend Steinhauser. On 27 November 1854 he set out for Harar and, with great difficulty, reached it with a party on 2 January 1855. They were admitted to see the Emir and permitted to stay until they decided to leave, mercifully unmolested, on 13 January. Burton then returned to Aden but went back to Berbera and was with John Hanning Speke and others when they were surrounded by unfriendly natives who attacked them. Burton used his sabre and Speke a pair of revolvers. In the course of fighting the raiders off, one of Burton's party was killed and Burton's face was run right through with a javelin, leaving distinctive scarring. Unsurprisingly, the party returned to Aden.

Burton's injuries were such that he had to return to England. He read his paper on Harar to the RGS on 11 June 1855 and received the gold medal, but he had let the grass grow under his feet in relation to the Hajj pilgrimage and his exploration of Somalia. Moreover, public attention was centred on the Crimean War and so he volunteered for service. Burton joined General Beatson's force of Bashi Bazouks in Constantinople but they did not see service, and again, Burton returned to England on 18 October 1855.

In August 1856, Burton met Isabel in the Botanical Gardens and courted her for a fortnight. Eventually, he proposed:

'You won't chalk up 'Mother will be angry' now I hope,' said Burton.
'Perhaps not,' replied Miss Arundell, 'but she will be all the same.'

She was too. Burton had a reputation for wildness and it did not go down well with respectable, Roman Catholic, English mothers. Marriage was postponed under parental objection. However, Isabel gave Burton a medal of the Virgin Mary which, along with several other amulets, he carried on all his travels. Quite a bit later, of course, they *did* marry.

Burton started devising his great plan to find the source of the River Nile which he supposed (correctly) was in the believed great lakes of central Africa. He was supported all round and given paid leave from the East India Company. He ('Dick') and John ('Jack') Hanning Speke were to lead the expedition and they arrived in Zanzibar on 20 December 1856 to make preparations. Burton observed:

'One of the gladdest moments in human life is the departing upon a distant journey into unknown lands. Shaking off with one effort the fetters of habit, the leaden weight of routine, the slavery of civilisation.'

However, he left a written declaration of love for Isabel.

Speke was born in 1821, the son of an army officer and Devonshire land owner, and was also of an imposing physical appearance.

The two made preliminary expeditions and Burton made copious notes and even prepared a book manuscript about Zanzibar. They sailed to Kaole on 17 June 1857 and started inland with one hundred bearers. As ever, Africa proved inhospitable to adventurers and they became ill. They stopped at Tabora on 7 November 1856 for one month to gather themselves. Burton got worse and could not walk for a year. He later claimed that on the way he had summarily executed a man who had just been discussing killing him and even blew up a group of conspirators with gunpowder! On 13 February 1858 they struck Lake Tanganyika – brilliant blue 'in the lap of its steel-coloured mountains'– and they sailed around it. On 26 May they went back to Tabora where Burton took to studying local languages and customs, whereas Speke wanted to try to explore further north for another lake. Burton stayed behind. Speke found Lake Victoria which was only later 'unveiled as Isis', the source of the River Nile. He returned to Tabora, ill with a delirium called 'Little Irons', and Burton nursed him through it. Then it was back to Zanzibar on 4 March, where Burton discovered the loss of his notes and manuscript. They then sailed for Aden on 22 March.

Speke arrived back in England on 9 May 1859 and went straight to the RGS to organise another expedition without Burton. The RGS gave him Captain James A. Grant. Speke also gave a lecture at Burlington House and when Burton arrived on 21 May, he found that, against his word, Speke had stolen a march on him. However, Burton wrote in his diary, about finding Lake Tanganyika: 'I have built me a monument stronger than brass.'

On 22 May 1860 Isabel was waiting in the house of a friend when she heard Burton's voice saying, 'I want Miss Arundell's address'. They then saw each other, rushed into each other's arms and went off and drove around in a cab.

Burton was ravaged by illness at this time and resembled a mummy rather than an adventurer. Isabel's father seemed impressed by him and at last consented to marriage, but Isabel's mother remained resolutely against him.

Burton decided to leave the matter for the time being and went off to Salt Lake City where he spent a period observing the Mormon community and speaking with one of its leaders, Brigham Young. Burton then went to San Francisco and returned to England via Panama. Arriving at Christmas 1860, Mrs Arundell finally agreed that the thirty-year-old Isabel could marry the forty-year-old Burton. They were wed at the Bavarian Catholic Church, Warwick Street, on 22 January 1861. From then on, Isabel called Burton 'Dick' or 'Jimmy'. They were taken up by Monckton Milnes (Lord Houghton) and brought into society through being hosted by Lord Palmerston. They met such people as the important poet A. C. Swinburne (they were both early admirers of Edward FitzGerald's translation of the *Rubáiyát of Omar Khayyám*), and the writer Thomas Carlyle. Lady Russell had Isabel presented at Court.

Now Burton and Isabel expected some reward for all his efforts, but alas, the best that Lord Russell, as Foreign Secretary, could produce was the consulship of Fernando Po at £700 a year. Still, he took it, grumbling: 'It is the old tale, England breeds great men, but grudges them opportunities for the manifestation of their greatness.' Burton went there on 24 August 1861 and Isabel stayed behind, owing to the dangers of the place. Burton knew that Richard Lander had not been the first or the last explorer to find a grave there.

He arrived on 26 September and used the healthiest spot he could find up in the hills as a sanatorium. Fortunately, he did not fall ill in Fernando Po. From here too he explored near parts of Africa, especially the Cameroon country and wrote his trips up as *Two Trips to Gorilla Land*. He came across the Fan cannibals and even saw the king's eldest daughter lead a dance. Seeing the gorillas he decided that they were not as terrible as they had been described.

Burton got a home leave, arrived in England at Christmas 1862 and spent his time with Isabel. On 6 January 1863, with James Hunt, he founded the Anthropological Society of London (which merged with the Ethnological Society in 1871 and became the Anthropological Institute of Great Britain). However, its original purpose, to enable the collection of arcane knowledge including sexual practices, seems to have been frustrated by what Burton called 'Mrs Grundy'. Burton returned to Fernando Po via Madeira, where he left Isabel. During the time he was posted to Fernando Po they met on Tenerife.

Lady Hester Lucy Stanhope (1776–1839).

Sir James Brooke KCB, DCL (Oxon), White Rajah of Sarawak (1803–1868), from an original portrait by Francis Grant, RA.

Richard Lemon Lander (1804–1834).

Mary Seacole (1805–1881).

Jane Elizabeth Digby (1807–1881), from an original portrait by Joseph Karl Stieler.

Colonel John Whitehead Peard, 'Garibaldi's Englishman' (1811–1880).

General Sir James Abbott KCB (1807–1896), from an original portrait by B. Baldwin.

Sir Richard Francis Burton KCMG (1821–1890), from an original portrait by Sir Frederick Leighton, RA.

John William Colenso, 1st Anglican Bishop of Natal (1814–1883).

John Hanning Speke (1827–1864), by Thomas Rodger.

Sir Thomas Johnstone Lipton Bart. KCVO (1850–1931).

Emily Hobhouse (1860–1926).

Mary Henrietta Kingsley (1862–1900).

Sir Francis Edward Younghusband KCSI, KCIE (1863–1942).

Colonel Percy Harrison Fawcett (1867–1925), from a photograph by Pelecchuco

(Robert) Peter Fleming OBE (1907–1971).

Gertrude Margaret Lowthian Bell CBE (1868–1926).

George Herbert Leigh Mallory (1886–1924) and Ruth Mallory.

Andrew Comyn Irvine (1902–1924) (left).

Dame Freya Madeline Stark DBE
(ca. 1893–1993).

Sir Francis Charles Chichester KBE (1901–1972).

Gladys May Aylward (1902–1970).

Amy Johnson CBE (1902–1941).

Sir Fitzroy Hew Royle Maclean Bart. KT, CBE (1911–1996).

Krystyna Skarbek–Granville (Christine Granville) GM, OBE, Croix de Guerre (ca. 1908–1952).

Tenzing Norgay GM (1914–1986), from the 'Mount Everest' photograph by Edmund Hillary.

Noor-un-Nisa Inayat Khan GC, MBE, Croix de Guerre (1914–1944).

Violette Reine Elizabeth Szabo GC, MBE, Croix de Guerre (1921–1945).

In November 1863 Burton was commissioned by the government to take presents to Gelele, King of Dahomey, to try to persuade him to cease human sacrifice and the slave trade. He left Fernando Po on 29 November 1863 by ship, for Whydah, the port of Dahomey, and waited for royal command to see the king. He then travelled to Kama where he saw the female bodyguard of one thousand Amazons. Gelele received him kindly and Burton was then accommodated at Abomey, the capital. He delivered the presents from Queen Victoria on 28 December. Various 'customs' then began, including slaughter of criminals and prisoners of war (which Burton refused to witness). Things were such in this savage place that, when the king died, up to five hundred wives and attendants went with him. Similar customs prevailed for lesser degrees of men and human life on this earth was regarded as cheap. Burton utterly failed in his mission but, strangely, seems to have come away with a favourable impression and defended the society on the basis that British society also countenanced needless loss of life.

In August 1864 he was granted leave again and by the end of the month he was in Liverpool. He learned that Speke's second expedition was supposed to have proved that Lake Victoria was the source of the Nile. Burton still did not accept this and tempers were running high. Public interest was great and so, egged on by manipulators, Burton agreed to an open debate with Speke at a British Association for the Advancement of Science meeting at Bath.

On 16 September 1864 Burton was on the platform, ready to start, when the President of the association suddenly announced that Speke would be a 'no show', as he had died in a shooting accident shortly before, while out bagging game. Old warrior Burton was greatly affected and went home and wept like a child.

The official version was that Speke had climbed a wall with his gun cocked and that it had gone off accidentally. Burton and others suspected that Speke had killed himself and, indeed, owing to the length of the guns of the time, it would be exceedingly difficult to *accidentally* shoot oneself with a shotgun. Maybe Speke, after stealing so much of Burton's thunder, just could not bear a public showdown. Burton wrote: 'The charitable say that he shot himself, the uncharitable say that I shot him.'

In fact, as the world now knows (by Stanley and Livingstone and others), the Nile does indeed rise in Lake Victoria (as Speke has postulated), and not (as maintained by Burton), in Lake Tanganyika. However, the world should not forget that the first expedition which Burton had devised and led, had been his master-plan and Speke had simply developed Burton's idea for 'unveiling Isis'.

As a result of Isabel's lobbying, Burton did not return to Fernando Po in September 1864 but was posted to Santos in Brazil. However, they preferred spending time in São Paulo and Rio de Janeiro where they were taken up by Emperor Dom Pedro II and his Empress. The Emperor was a student of the East and found much to discuss with Burton. On one occasion, the Emperor was so engrossed with Burton's conversation that he kept banquet guests waiting half an hour. The Empress gave Isabel a fine diamond bracelet and Burton gave a lecture before the Emperor.

Burton's friend Steinhauser, (with whom he had discussed translating *The Arabian Nights*), died in July 1866, causing Burton much pain. The Burtons later visited a deep mine in Minas Gerais. One bigger adventure that Burton had was to descend the fifteen-hundred-mile-long São Françisco river. However, Burton fell ill and was granted sick leave. Isabel returned to lobby for a healthier posting and Burton undertook a tour of South America. He was in Peru when he learned that he had, at last, been posted to Damascus and he returned to England in June 1869. Before he took up his new posting he entertained a European tour with his friend Swinburne.

The posting to Damascus was Burton's dream come true. Here too, he practised disguise to go amongst the local people, but unfortunately, the Consul-General in Beirut did not like him and the Ambassador at Constantinople undermined him. The Pasha of Syria was also hostile. Burton did not curry much favour when he refused to help Jewish money-lenders and leading British Jews called him anti-Semitic so, by the spring of 1871, he was on the transfer list. Then he shot himself in the foot by trying to give protection to a Muslim mystical group and the Ottoman Empire demanded that he be recalled. The Burtons' friendship and interaction in Damascus with Jane Digby has already been related. He left on 18 August 1871 and had to wait for another appointment. He wrote as always but then he was sponsored to go prospecting for sulphur in Iceland during the summer of 1872.

Burton was posted to Trieste on 24 October 1872 and found that he had much leisure and much leave. He made a translation of the Portuguese poet Luiz Vaz de Camões's *Lusiads* in 1880 and with Foster FitzGerald Arbuthnot, started on eastern erotic texts. For this purpose, they formed the Kama Shastra Society in 1882 and produced the *Kama Sutra* (1883), *Ananga Ranga* (1885) and *The Perfumed Garden of Cheikh Nefzaoui* (1886). Besides all that, in 1875 the Burtons went to India. Burton started his translation of *The Thousand Arabian Nights and The One Night* in 1882, keeping in the ribaldry, mischief and sex, and building on his widely collected knowledge for footnotes. It has been wondered what the many Bishops, padding through the library of the Athenaeum Club in London, might have thought had they but known the type of thing that Burton was translating at the large round table there.

Eventually, the Burtons published the sixteen-volume translation themselves (1885–1888), incurring the large expense of £6,000 and limiting the print run to a thousand copies– but they made a profit of £10,000 from it and, at last, Burton had a significant commercial success in the realm of literature.

Very briefly, the *Nights* is about the tales that Shaharazad told her husband, the king, to save her life, after he resolved to kill each wife after one night of marriage. She always withheld the ending of the tales, and after one thousand and one nights her life was spared. As A. S. Byatt has said, the tales are full of mischief, valour, ribaldry and romance. Some of them have become very well known: *Alaeddin, or The Wonderful Lamp* , *Sinbad the Seaman and Sinbad the Landsman* , and *Ali Baba and The Forty Thieves* .

In 1884 Burton published *The Book of The Sword* – and suffered his first heart attack.

In 1886 he was made a Knight Commander of the Order of St Michael and St George, but was refused early retirement. One of Burton's pet projects at this time was to translate from the Arabic what he had rendered in *The Perfumed Garden*, but this time he called it *The Scented Garden*. He had practically finished the first part of this for publication when he died.

By October 1890 Burton's health was failing. On 19 October a bird pecked three times on a window of their home and Burton remarked that it was a sign of death. At 9.30 pm he retired to his room and Isabel read him some prayers. A dog began to howl, which the superstitious (and Isabel) regard as another harbinger of death. Burton read a book for a while and developed a pain in his foot. He was evidently dying and Isabel called Dr Baker. Burton's breathing became very laboured and then he said, 'I am dying; I am dead', and Isabel held him in her arms. Despite the fact that Burton was dead before the priest arrived and that he was not a Roman Catholic, Isabel insisted on Extreme Unction being administered to him, and his body, covered with the scars of his many fights, was then embalmed.

There were three funerals in Trieste but none of them resulted in burial. Instead, Isabel had Burton installed in a private chapel. Every flag in Trieste was at half-mast and multitudes thronged the streets for him; every head uncovered and the press of the world rang with his praises. Swinburne wrote an elegy and Isabel responded in a very strange way – by burning many of his private papers, including the manuscript of *The Scented Garden*, to 'protect his memory', despite the fact she felt it was his *magnum opus*.

Maybe, owing to grief, she did not really know what she was doing or why. However, she did, by the administration of Extreme Unction and the destruction of his notes and manuscripts, alienate some of Burton's friends.

Nine months after he died, Burton was interred in Mortlake cemetery in Surrey, beneath a marble representation of an Arab tent. Six years later, Isabel joined him.

As a natural linguist and inspired translator, intrepid explorer, curious anthropologist and fact-gatherer, Richard Francis Burton is probably without peer in the history of England.

Chapter 10

Sir Thomas Johnstone Lipton, 1st Bart. KCVO (1850–1931)

'I always fear that creation will expire before teatime.'

Sydney Smith

JOHN FIELD, British High Commissioner to Sri Lanka, said in 1992: 'It can be said of very few individuals that their labours have helped to shape the landscape of a country. But the beauty of the hill country as it now appears owes much to the inspiration of James Taylor, the man who introduced tea cultivation to Sri Lanka.' Taylor had arrived to work at the Lodecondera coffee plantation in 1852.

Up until the 1860s coffee and the cinchona tree comprised the principal cultivation in Ceylon. From the bark of the cinchona tree is derived quinine, which was in demand in the fight to keep malaria at bay. Now, largely thanks to two men, James Taylor and Sir Thomas Lipton, Sri Lanka (still producing 'Ceylon' tea), is the world's greatest tea exporter. In 1866 the coffee plantation for which James Taylor worked sent an employee to India to learn about tea production. The result of a favourable visit and study was the bringing of tea seeds to Ceylon. Taylor planted them in an original tea garden of just nineteen acres and some of the original trees are still producing tea.

Taylor started leaf processing, rolling the tea by hand and firing the leaves (to stabilise the enzymes) in clay stoves on charcoal fires; the leaves hanging in wire trays. In the light of what happened next, this was all very much a preparation for the consequences of a catastrophe in the coffee plantations.

From 1869 a fungus killed off the coffee trees in Ceylon and eventually the land was used to grow tea. By 1872 there was a bigger processing plant on the Lodecondera estate, including machines for rolling the tea. In 1875 the first Ceylon tea was sent to the London tea auctions, and one million packets were sold at the Chicago World's Fair in 1893.

Owing to the crash in coffee production, land was cheap. Seeing the potential, a Scottish-born, self-made grocer, called Thomas Johnstone Lipton, bought up four estates to plant tea and take his 'Brisk' tea 'from the tea garden to the teapot' without the middlemen. This brought down the price, enabling poorer people to enjoy the great British cup of tea which Lipton was singularly responsible for introducing across the range of the social spectrum.

Lipton was born in Glasgow on 10 May ca. 1850, the son of Thomas Lipton senior and his wife Frances, both of Irish descent. His father was a labourer who eventually opened a small grocery shop in Glasgow; apparently specialising in buttons and eggs! When he was nine, Lipton worked in the shop as an errand boy. At the age of eleven he went to work in a stationery shop and after that, for a shirt-maker and then as a cabin boy on Belfast steamers. He travelled to the USA in 1865 with one pound and ten shillings in his pocket and worked as a labourer on a Virginia tobacco plantation and then as an accounts clerk in South Carolina. Despite the lack of an extended formal education, he seems, with some later night-school tuition, to have been perfectly literate and numerate from an early age. Lipton worked his way from Charleston to New York on board a ship where he had begun his voyage as a stowaway. Aged twenty, he worked in a large grocery store in New York where he gained valuable experience in retail sales. He then returned to Glasgow with five-hundred dollars of savings.

For a time he returned to work in his father's shop but their ideas were quite different. Thomas Jr wanted to expand, whereas his father cautiously demurred. Accordingly, aged twenty-one years and with his hundred pounds, Lipton set out to build his trading empire. He opened the first shop in Stobcross Street, Glasgow. He brought in food direct from the suppliers in Ireland and his 'Irish Markets' cut out the middlemen, drove down prices and presented serious challenge to the competition.

By the time that he was twenty-four years old, Lipton had a second shop in the High Street and others quickly followed; bigger, better, cleaner, cheaper, with smart, diligent counter staff. He backed it all up with an advertising campaign: advertisements on walls of buildings and his own branded packaging. Eventually, he even made his own packaging and started to diversify with an operation in the USA.

By 1888, his stores reached London and, already a millionaire by the age of thirty, Lipton moved there in 1889, eventually buying a house called Osidge, in Southgate, from where he travelled to work by carriage. He also visited Ceylon on a voyage to Australia and saw the merit in buying tea plantations in the hills of Ceylon, thus cutting out the middlemen and the London tea auctions which enabled him to lower the price and bring about a mass appeal:

'Millions drink it daily: Lipton's delicious teas'.

Lipton built the Dambatenne Tea Factory in 1890 with the best of everything and accommodating 1,600 workers and their families: 4,000 people in all. The motto was John Ruskin's expression: *'Quality is no accident. It is the result of intelligent effort.'*

'Lipton's seat' is still a viewing place, high up with glorious views, at Dambetenne, in the Poonagala Hills, Haputale, where he would go to contemplate on his visits to the island.

Lipton even invested in research in his tea-tasting house to package teas that were most compatible with the water of the localities where it was to be sold. This was a much broader operation than that of Fortnum & Mason which provided a similar service for individual customers.

By 1897, he had made his empire and, although he did not neglect it, (he remained Life President after he eventually sold out the store business in 1927), he devoted much of his time and resources to philanthropy and international yacht racing (in which he made a considerable impression) as well as gaining the friendship of the Prince of Wales (later Edward VII) and George V, themselves both keen yachtsmen.

In 1897 (Victoria's Diamond Jubilee), Alexandra, Princess of Wales, became involved in a scheme to feed the poor but was seriously short of the funding. Lipton stumped up twenty-five thousand pounds of his own. A little later, Alexandra became Patron of dining facilities, again for poor people, and he funded the whole operation at a cost of one hundred thousand pounds. Perhaps, unsurprisingly, Lipton was knighted in 1898 and then also formed the company Lipton Ltd. Balancing philanthropy with pleasure, he bought a steam yacht which he called (maybe echoing his Irish roots), *Erin*, used for entertaining on a lavish scale.

Lipton had been fascinated by sailing since his first early voyage to the United States of America, and as soon as he could, (in 1899) he challenged for the America's Cup with his sailing yacht *Shamrock*. Using a professional crew, he challenged again and again for thirty years but never won anything except acknowledgement of his sportsmanship and excellent publicity for his business.

The America's Cup is the oldest trophy in international sport and dates from 1851. A schooner, called *America*, owned by a syndicate from the New York Yacht Club, sailed past the Royal Yacht, from where Queen Victoria was watching a race in the Solent and it dipped its ensign thrice in salute. Queen Victoria asked who was second in the race and the reply was, 'There is no second, ma'am'. The *America* won the Royal Yacht Squadron's hundred-pound cup and took it back in triumph to America. The schooner's owners then donated the cup to the New York Yacht Club under a deed of gift which provides that the trophy has to be a perpetual challenge cup for friendly competition between nations. Since then only four nations have won the trophy.

Shamrock IV took the first two races in 1920 but *Resolute* won the next three. Lipton's final challenge came in 1930 with *Shamrock V* , which lost four straight races to *Enterprise*. Harold Vanderbilt, who had skippered the winning yacht afterwards said:

'Uppermost in our minds is a feeling of sympathy for that grand old sportsman, Sir Thomas Lipton, with whom our relations have been so pleasant. This is perhaps his last attempt to lift the America's Cup. The ambition of a lifetime, to achieve which he has spent millions, is perhaps never to be realised. It has been our duty to shut the door in his face. In defeat lies the test of true sportsmanship, and he has proved to be a wonderful sportsman, quite the finest it has ever been our good fortune to race against.'

Then the American people presented Lipton with a gold cup in honour of his sportsmanship and good humour. Kept out for so long by snobbery against his roots in 'trade', just before he died he was at last admitted to the Royal Yacht Squadron. He is a member of the America's Cup Hall of Fame.

He had been advanced to Knight Commander of the Royal Victorian Order in 1901, and in 1902 was created a baronet, prompting the then Prime Minister, Lord Salisbury to blurt out 'My grocer is being made a baronet!'

In 1909 Lipton was also made a Knight Commander of the Grand Order of the Crown of Italy and presented the Italians with a cup to be used for an international football competition. The Football Association, for some odd reason, declined to nominate a team so Lipton turned to West Auckland Town to represent Britain. The team was made up mostly of local coal miners but they beat Red Star of Zurich and Juventus to win this cup in 1910 and successfully defended the title in 1911. Because of this, Lipton is often credited with initiating the first international football trophy tournament.

Lipton held an honorary military title and in the First World War, he sent *Erin* on missions to deliver medical supplies until she was sunk.

Sir Thomas Lipton died at his London home on 2 October 1931 and was buried next to his parents in Glasgow. Unmarried (although never short of ladies), he left his fortune to Glasgow charities.

As a little aside, in honour of their former customer Sir Thomas Lipton (who, large, rangy and genial, was the archetypical Edwardian man about town), the French shirt-maker Charvet makes a 'Lipton' bow tie to this very day. It is large and covered in polka dots, maybe reminiscent of this big-hearted, flamboyant, innovative, sporting, British tradesman.

'Lipton's Tea' is still a brand name all over the world.

Chapter 11

Emily Hobhouse (1860–1926)

'I came quite naturally, in obedience to the feeling of unity or oneness of womanhood... it is when the community is shaken to its foundations, that abysmal depths of privation call to each other and that a deeper unity of humanity evinces itself.'

Emily Hobhouse, on the conditions that she found in British concentration camps for women and children, in South Africa.

EMILY HOBHOUSE was born on 9 April 1860 at St Ive, near Liskeard, in east Cornwall. She was the fifth of six children of Reginald Hobhouse, rector of St Ive and Archdeacon of Bodmin, Cornwall, and his wife, Caroline (née Salusbury-Trelawny). Caroline's uncle was Arthur, Baron Hobhouse, who was later to support her financially through her adventures and campaigns.

Emily was educated at home by her mother and governesses, with a term in 1876 at a school in London. She remained at home caring for her parents, especially her ill father, and doing local parish work.

However, after her father's death in 1895, Emily decided, quite unexpectedly, to go America and Mexico and undertake charitable work among the Cornish miners who had emigrated as a result of the crash in the home mining industry.

First, she went to the mining town of Virginia, Minnesota, where she found that the few Cornish miners there had little need of her charity. Accordingly, she turned her attention to mission welfare and temperance projects.

Emily Hobhouse appears, both in her writing and in her pictures, to have been as brisk as a cup of Lipton's tea, but she seems to have entered into an engagement to marry an American businessman, called John Carr Jackson and they bought a ranch together in Mexico. However, maybe she caught him with a bottle of Jim Beam whiskey because the engagement was broken off. When the ranch failed and she was short of cash, Emily returned to England in 1898. However, her commitment to the idea of marriage is demonstrated by the fact that she had got as far as buying her wedding dress.

Plainly in need of a cause all her life, Emily became interested in the struggle for female emancipation, and in November 1898, was elected to the council of the Women's Industrial Council, working as an investigator for the Council and producing reports on child labour.

In 1900 she was instrumental in a scheme to set up a company providing housing for 'educated working women' in London, and although she supported the women's suffrage movement, she did not approve of the extremist means of the suffragettes. Indeed, in such respects, Emily Hobhouse seems to have been socially conservative.

Following the outbreak of the Second Boer War, on 11 October 1899, Emily became a member of the South African Conciliation Committee, which was launched on 1 November 1899. Leonard Courtney (Baron Courtney of Penwith), a former liberal politician, was its president. Emily was the honorary secretary of its women's branch, formed early in 1900. To initial, general public annoyance, she organised a number of protests against the war.

However, public opinion turned during 1900 when reports reached Britain of the British army's brutality in driving Boer women and children from their houses and farms to be housed in displaced persons' camps which have been described as the basic templates for the later, notorious Nazi concentration camps. As she later said:

'Above all one would hope that the good sense, if not the mercy, of the English people, will cry out against the further development of this cruel system, which falls with crushing effect upon the old, the weak, and the children.'

She established the South African Women and Children's Distress Fund to collect money to help the Boer women and children. She even went to South Africa, in December 1900, to investigate the situation for herself and to distribute funds. She managed to get permission to visit some of the concentration camps and spent many weeks in the Orange River and Cape colonies.

Emily saw the appalling conditions which resulted from lack of proper accommodation, food and water and sanitation. Disease and death lurked all around. She did what she could to raise awareness of the situation and improve it, and then returned to England in May 1901.

Emily happened to travel on the same ship as Sir Alfred Milner, the British High Commissioner to South Africa, to whom she had a letter of introduction. He told her that he had received many reports of her activities.

She campaigned to draw public attention in Britain to the conditions in South Africa, especially the conditions in the camps. She had exchanges with members of the British government (under Conservative Prime Minister, Lord Salisbury), notably, St John Brodrick and Joseph Chamberlain (who both saw her as presenting a general threat to Empire), and she published her report to the South African Distress Fund in June 1901.

The leader of the Liberal opposition to the government, Sir Henry Campbell-Bannerman, asked in a speech on 14 June: 'When is a war not a war? When it is carried on by methods of barbarism in South Africa'. The publication of Emily's report (*Report of a Visit to the Camps of Women and Children in the Cape and Orange River Colonies*), was delivered to the British government in June 1901. She had become a thorn in the side of the administration of the day. But the government did then appoint six women as a committee of inquiry into the camps which was presided over by (Dame) Millicent Fawcett (a prominent feminist and a founder of Newnham College, Cambridge (a college for women). Thanks to Emily, conditions in some of the camps (in which an estimated twenty-six thousand women and children died), improved. Even so, the Fawcett committee, from which Emily was expressly excluded, shared her opinion about the lack of suitable accommodation and the poor organisation of the camps, and their Parliamentary report, published in February 1902, backed the recommendations that she had made the year before.

When Emily tried to re-enter South Africa in November 1901, Lord Kitchener, who described her as 'That bloody woman', forcibly turned her around on a troop ship and sent her back. Even so, Kitchener stopped the furtherance of the concentration camps.

The War ended on 31 May 1902 and Emily was able to return to South Africa in 1903, when she was instrumental in various resettlement and rehabilitation projects, including the establishment of technical schools for lace-making, spinning, and weaving.

In 1907 she was appointed to manage funding for the schools in South Africa but this was shortly taken over by the new governments in South Africa, and Emily, her portrait hanging in the Pretoria Museum of Cultural History, returned in broken health to Europe where she lived quietly in Italy until the outbreak of the First World War. At this point, she worked for the

International Women's Movement For Peace in Amsterdam before travelling through Belgium and Germany in 1916, inspecting conditions of refugees and prisoners of war. She even met the German Foreign Minister, avoiding internment for herself, and returned to England to organise exchanges of prisoners of war, amid cries of treason.

After the end of the war, Emily set up a relief fund for German children, called 'The Fund to Aid Swiss Relief' which was later absorbed into the Save the Children Fund in 1919. She even found time to be chairwoman of the Russian Babies' Fund.

In the autumn of 1919 she went to Austria as a representative of the Save the Children Fund, made a report on conditions in Vienna and Leipzig and organised local administration. It is a testament to her dynamic force that, for this, she was honoured by the city of Leipzig and the German Red Cross. A bust of her was even placed in the administration building of Leipzig; a copy being sent to the war museum in Bloemfontein.

In 1921 Emily moved back to Cornwall – St Ives – in the far west. She lived in a house bought for her by public subscriptions raised by Afrikaners, but she soon returned to London where she wrote of her experiences, some of which were published at the time and others left as manuscripts to be published after her death.

Emily Hobhouse died of pleurisy in London on 8 June 1926, probably exhausted by all her exertions carried out regardless of the criticism which she so often encountered in Britain and at the hands of its Establishment.

Her body was cremated and the ashes taken to South Africa where, in October 1926, and already an honorary citizen of South Africa, she was accorded a state funeral. According to one account, she was 'buried like a princess', in a part of the Bloemfontein war memorial, called the National Women's Monument, designed after a sketch by Emily herself. The only others buried at the war memorial are President Steyn and his wife, the Rev D. J. Kestell and General de Wet.

There is a town and several streets named after her in South Africa but, so far as I know, Emily Hobhouse also enjoys the singular distinction amongst pacifists of having had a nuclear-powered war submarine originally named after her.

Also, so far as I know, the best memorials to her in her native Cornwall are John Hall's splendid biography of her published by Truran Books, and a private plaque in the Porthminster Hotel, in St Ives.

Chapter 12

Mary Henrietta Kingsley (1862–1900)

'He prayeth best, who loveth best
All things both great and small;
For the dear God who loveth us,
He made and loveth all.'

From *The Rime of The Ancient Mariner*
by Samuel Taylor Coleridge

MARY HENRIETTA Kingsley was born in Islington, London, on 13 October 1862, the eldest child of George Henry Kingsley, doctor and traveller, and his wife Mary (née Bailey). Her paternal uncles were the writers Charles and Henry Kingsley.

In 1863 the family moved to Highgate where her brother was born in 1866. Her father favoured employment as the private physician to rich, titled families on their European and world tours and was often away. He was even nearly a member of a party of exploration that was to have gone with General Custer when he was cornered and slaughtered by Sitting Bull and his warriors at Little Big Horn between 25–26 June 1876.

Mary was a quiet and solitary girl who received little formal education and taught herself from the books, especially those on travel and anthropology, which she found at home. She even learned German so that she could read some of them.

In 1879 the family moved first to Bexleyheath, Kent, and then, in 1886, to Cambridge, where Mary's brother, Charles, had gone up to Christ's College to read law. Here Mary made friends in academia, including Francis Burkitt and Agnes Smith Lewis. In 1888 Lucy Toulmin Smith took Mary to Paris for a week and gave her a taste for travel.

Following this, Mary had to devote herself to nursing her mother whose health declined so rapidly that she was eventually completely paralysed. Later,

Mary also had to care for her father who had returned home ill after a bout of rheumatic fever. He died in February 1892, and her mother died the following April, leaving Mary with reasonable independent means. She was now freed from the tremendous burdens of personal care and embarked on a trip to the Canary Islands in August, which did her a power of good in mind, body and spirit.

In the Canaries, Mary also had some glimpses of African goods from the country about which she had already read so much.

Back in England, Mary and her brother moved to a flat in Addison Road, Kensington, but she thought about travel and of furthering the anthropological studies which she had begun in books. India was her first choice but then she decided to go to West Africa. She sent letters of introduction to missionaries, traders, and government officials there and set out in August 1893.

She landed in Freetown, Sierra Leone, on 17 August, and made her way south to Luanda. After her return to the north in October, she travelled to Richard Dennett's trading station at Cabinda. Information gathered on this two-week visit later appeared in the introduction to Dennett's *Notes on the Folk Lore of the Fjort, French Congo*. Mary also collected various scientific specimens along her route. She returned to England in December 1893.

The scientific collections she brought back were esteemed by the scientific community.

Mary decided to start with more organised research in West Africa and sought advice from Dr Albert Günther, the curator of zoology at the British Museum. By the end of the year she was commissioned by Macmillan for a book on West Africa. She sailed on 23 December 1894 with Lady Ethel Macdonald, the wife of the Commissioner-General of the Oil Rivers Protectorate and stayed with the Macdonalds at the Calabar residency for four months, engaged in helping to nurse the European residents through an outbreak of smallpox and making excursions inland. She also accompanied the Macdonalds on an official visit to the Spanish Governor of the island of Fernando Po. In the April she went upstream to Ekene to visit a missionary called Mary Slessor, with whom she became friends; one of the few missionaries of whom Mary approved.

At the beginning of May, Mary went south towards Gabon, up the Ogooué River and through the rapids above N'Djolé. She even went over a part of the Fang country which had never been penetrated by a European before, and she led her own canoe expedition from Lambarene on the Ogooué River to Agonjo on the upper waters of the Ramboë River.

In the August she visited Corisco Island and went up Mount Cameroun. Not only all this, she even traded in rubber, ivory, tobacco, and other goods.

She also made a collection of insects, shells, and plants; eighteen species of reptiles; and sixty-five species of fish, of which three were entirely new and were named for her.

Mary arrived back in England on 30 November 1895. There was great public and press interest in her and her extraordinary, solitary travels and, although she protested about being described as a 'New Woman', she responded positively to requests for articles and lectures.

In February 1896 she delivered her first lecture to the Scottish Geographical Society, through a male fellow of the Society, in her presence. In March her paper to the Liverpool Geographical Society was read out by the trader James Irvine. By now she was proposing a system of informal economic imperialism in Africa.

In January 1897 Mary's first book, *Travels in West Africa, Congo Français, Corisco and Cameroons*, was published as a miscellany of facts, information and opinion. As a result, she met even more influential people, including a businessman called John Holt and the famed anthropologist James Frazer.

Sierra Leone had been declared a British protectorate in 1896 and the British sought to impose a hut tax, like a kind of local authority tax, for administration. The tax charge was calculated according to hut size. This provoked rebellion, principally by Temne Chief Bai Bureh and the Mende led by Momoh Jah. Hundreds of men on the African and British sides died in the fighting that followed. Mary Kingsley's article on the tax in *The Spectator* of 19 March 1898 brought her into political controversy. Joseph Chamberlain (father of Austin and Neville) was the Colonial Secretary and he secretly sought Mary's advice. However, by this time, she was suffering from exhaustion and entered a nervous breakdown from which she took some time to recover.

Over the next two years Mary lectured on West Africa across Britain to a range of different audiences. Her aim was to enlighten the general British public. She spoke in favour of British trading interests but condemned the injustices of the Crown Colony system. Maybe surprisingly, she also defended the 'liquor traffic' which had, less surprisingly, been condemned by the missionary societies.

Mary claimed that she was able to 'think in black'. Like John William Colenso before her (and for similar reasons), she defended polygamy and, maybe most surprisingly, even the slave trade (which had its roots in African society). She opposed the attempts by Europeans to impose their cultures and values on the Africans and from her we get references to something close to deprecation of 'white trash culture'.

In her own writing, she concentrated on the Fang Africans who were still, as she put it 'in the raw state'. They are an aggressive, warrior tribe, follow ancestor worship and carry the bones of their ancestors in boxes. Down to the seventeenth century, they had put the bones of their enemies in the cooking pot.

It has been noted that Mary was not pretty and always wore dark clothes and pinned her hair back to create an impression of age and outward conformity that was at odds with her eccentric opinions. However, she had a keen sense of humour.

In February 1899 *West African Studies* was published. This was Mary's second book and went much further than the first, even outlining an 'alternative plan' for West Africa. Her idea was to remove administrative control from career civil servants and concentrate it in the hands of European trading interests, but having reference to African opinion on issues arising.

Her point was that the proposed system would leave African cultural, legal, and social organisations intact, while improving its economic infrastructure.

In February 1899 Mary met Matthew Nathan, the acting Governor of Sierra Leone. She fell in love with him, but not he with her.

Mary described herself as 'a bushman *and* a drawing-roomer', and, feeling the strain of so much effort, she longed to travel again. The Second Boer War breaking out in 1899 made her think of going to South Africa and then back to West Africa. She set off again on 11 March 1900. On her arrival at Cape Town she volunteered as a nurse and was sent to Simon's Town Palace Hospital to care for injured and typhoid-ridden Boer prisoners of war.

Eventually, typhoid fever claimed Mary and she died, tragically young on 3 June 1900, and was buried at sea.

Mary Kingsley approached the subject of African government and trade with an appeal for a hands-off policy towards African social and legal systems and customs which came to be called 'Kingsleyism'. As a result of her raising awareness of Africa, The Congo Reform Association was founded in 1904 to point out the appalling abuses which were taking place in Belgium's Free Congo State (leading to its annexation by Belgium in 1908). The African Society (now the Royal African Society) was also founded in Mary Kingsley's memory to continue her work.

Mary was undoubtedly ahead of her time in her thinking and her empathy for native Africans, but she was not really much of a feminist and condemned and derided them as '*androgynes*'. She is commemorated in The Mary Kingsley medal of the Liverpool School of Tropical Medicine.

Mary was undoubtedly an 'original' in her thinking; combining an odd mix of European paternalism and African cultural conservation in her approach to the practical problems posed by development of African trade. However, maybe one of the most remarkable things about her is that, although her actual knowledge of Africa as a real place was concentrated in such a small space of time, she managed both to have a real impact during her lifetime and to leave behind influential publications and lectures and an enduring framework for much later thinking and action.

Chapter 13

Sir Francis Edward Younghusband KCSI, KCIE (1863–1942)

'Make me feel the wild pulsation that I felt before the strife,
When I heard my days before me, and the tumult of my life.'
From the poem *Locksley Hall* by Alfred, Lord Tennyson

FRANCIS EDWARD Younghusband was, in the early part of his career, less typical of the liberal and interactive face of empire, which was exemplified by men such as James Abbott and John William Colenso, but he shares the right to be regarded as a great adventurer too. He also modified his views as he matured. Accordingly, if he falls to be judged at all, it should be according to the general values of his own time, race and class.

Younghusband was born on 31 May 1886, at Murree hill station in the Himalayan foothills (of what was then Kashmir), to Major John William Younghusband and Clara Jane (née Shaw). He was sent to Clifton College, where he made friends with the minor, but tub-thumping, imperial poet Henry Newbolt, who gave the world such jingoistic verses as those in his *Vitae Lampada*, which famously includes the verse:

> *The sand of the desert is sodden red, – -*
> *Red with the wreck of a square that broke; – -*
> *The Gatling's jammed and the Colonel dead,*
> *And the regiment blind with dust and smoke.*
> *The river of death has brimmed his banks,*
> *And England's far, and Honour a name,*
> *But the voice of a schoolboy rallies the ranks:*
> *'Play up! play up! and play the game!'*

After school, Younghusband was commissioned into the 1st King's Dragoon Guards in 1882 and stationed at Meerut.

His life's exploration was principally to shore up the empire which he so deeply believed to be a benign and paternalistic influence.

In 1886 he went on a seven-month mission to Manchuria. In Peking he met up with his commander and they decided to return to India by separate routes. Younghusband set out just with guides and crossed the Gobi desert to Hami and then went over the Himalayas to Kashmir. On the way, he crossed the Muztagh Pass, a feat which heightened his sense of purpose in exploration. Back in London in 1888, he lectured at the RGS and was awarded the Gold Medal in 1890. He wrote up his further explorations between 1889–1891 in India, Russia, China and Afghanistan in his book *Heart of a Continent,* in which he succinctly stated his belief in the merits of seeking travel and adventure:

> 'There are (those) whom I hope my book may reach —
> some few among those thousands and thousands who stay at
> home in England. Amongst these there are numbers who
> have that longing to go out and see the world which is the
> characteristic of Englishmen. It is not natural to an English-
> man to sit at an office desk, or spend his whole existence
> amid such tame excitement as life in London, and shooting
> partridges and pheasants afford. Many consider themselves
> tied down to home; but they often tie themselves down.
> And if a man has indeed the spirit of travel in him, nothing
> should be allowed to stand in the way of his doing as he
> wishes.
> And one of the hopes I have as I write this book is, that it
> may tempt some few among the stay-at-homes to go out and
> breathe a little of the pure fresh air of Nature, and inhale
> into their beings some of the revivifying force and
> heightened power of enjoyment of all that is on this earth
> which it can give.'

Younghusband's simple statement of a self-evident truth is as valid today as it was when it was written. Yet it seems that, if anything, it is even more difficult for today's youngsters to break free of the channelling and shackling of early life and the inculcation of the corrosive belief that the main aim of life is to play it safe in some quiet corner from which one is never likely to be called upon to 'stand up and let's see what you can really do!' The other principal aim of modern life, equally corrosive of the human spirit, seems to be to amass as much money as possible just to gloat upon it; with a long-shot for the very few who are chosen to be film stars, pop stars or international footballers or golfers.

There should be much more encouragement of the spirit of adventure and more awareness of President J. F. Kennedy's maxim: 'The only failure in life is not to aim too high and miss the mark but to aim too low and hit it.' It might also be noted in passing that, with one or two exceptions, most of the great adventurers in this book left very little in the way of cash and possessions. Lipton left the most but, even then, in his lifetime he had spent – and given away – many times the amount that he left. However, of the rest, they left a perpetual memorial in the fruits of their exploration and research. Moreover, several of them dispensed and even exhausted themselves in the service of others; from accruing and spreading knowledge of the world to nursing infirmity and standing up for the underdog.

Younghusband's sense of wonder at nature can be seen from this passage, in the same book, when he first sees the Pamir Mountains:

'*(We) emerged on to the great central plain of Turkestan again near Artysh.*
 From here I saw one of those sights
which almost strike one dumb at first — a line of snowy peaks
apparently suspended in mid-air. They were the Pamir
Mountains, but they were so distant, and the lower atmosphere
was so laden with dust, that their base was hidden, and only
their snowy summits were visible. One of these was over
twenty-five thousand feet high, and another twenty-two thou-
sand, while the spot where I stood was only four thousand;
so their height appeared enormous and greater still on account
of this wonderful appearance of being separated from earth.'

In 1891 Younghusband was appointed Commander of the Indian Empire and he held various administrative posts between 1892–1894. In 1895 he was *The Times* correspondent in relation to actions of the successful British Chitral relief force. This was sent after the fort at Chitral was besieged on 15 March 1895, as a result of a dispute over the succession to the local ruler (the Mehtar).

Younghusband was then appointed as *The Times* correspondent in

Rhodesia (now Zimbabwe) and the Transvaal and took part in the Jameson Raid. This was an insurgence between 29 December 1895 and 2 January 1896 when British colonial administrator Leander Starr Jameson used police to mount a raid on Paul Kruger's Transvaal Republic. The intended purpose was to inspire an insurrection by British workers there and produce a shift in the balance of power (they were the so-called 'Johannesburg conspirators'). The raid spectacularly failed to do anything except further sour Anglo-Boer relations. Younghusband later regretted his own involvement, even as a gentleman of the press.

On 11 August 1897 he married Helen Augusta Magniac, an MP's daughter, and they had one surviving child, a daughter (in whose household Gladys Aylward would later work).

In September 1898 Younghusband and his new wife were back in India. In November he was made British political agent at Deoli, and awarded the newly-created Kaisar-i-Hind gold medal for services to the Empire in 1900. In 1902 he was Resident in Indore and in 1903 was appointed as head of a mission to promote British interests in Tibet and to survey the country. He wildly exceeded his authority.

Younghusband went to Tibet in December 1903 with ten thousand men and advanced on Lhasa. On the way in 1904 there was a massacre of seven hundred Tibetans at Chumi Shengo which caused widespread horror and criticism. Younghusband rode into Lhasa in August and mistook his reception as a welcome. However, quite outside his instructions, he negotiated a treaty in September, giving Britain rights over the territory, which upset the Russians and later had to be renegotiated to placate them. By his actions Younghusband had created a bad odour and was rewarded with the award of the humble Knight Commander of the Indian Empire in 1904. He wrote a book about his exploits, called *India* and *Tibet* in 1910. Eventually, he was advanced (in 1917) to the higher degree of Knight Commander of the Star of India.

In 1905 Younghusband received honorary degrees from Cambridge and Edinburgh universities, and between 1906 to 1910 he was Resident in Kashmir. He returned to England in 1910. His Asian experiences are summed up in his two books, *The Light of Experience* and *But in Our Lives*. In 1912 he received an honorary degree from Bristol University. During the First World War, he organised news telegrams for India House, and in 1916 arranged the Fight for Right Society to urge on the War; the original anthem of which was William Blake's poem *Jerusalem*, set to music by Sir Hubert Parry in 1916. However, Parry withdrew his support for the ultrapatriotic movement in 1917 and the anthem was later taken up by the suffragettes, with Parry's approval.

Younghusband also founded, and then became Vice President of, the Royal Central Asian Society and chairman of the India Society.

Despite his earlier jingoism, he gradually advocated a gradual move towards Indian self-government after about 1930.

From 1910, he had become increasingly interested in religious and philosophical questions and wrote books on the subjects which combined the elements of various religions and science as well as linking mysticism and sex; his ideas were advancing towards the merits of combining western advancement and eastern spirituality. He then became involved in a whole raft of organisations touching on these subjects, such as the Aristotlelian Society, the League of Nations, and the Society for the Study of Religions. In 1936 he founded the World Congress of Faiths which still exists to promote better understanding between people of different faiths. Maybe it deserves more support. Younghusband saw the real divide as between those with a faith and those with none, rather than as between members of different faiths.

He saw mankind's problems as originating in rationalism, secularism and materialism. I am not convinced that the recent history of the world really bears him out on that.

A believer in the universality of religion, he was a communicating member of the Church of England, who nonetheless engaged with other faiths, especially on his travels.

In his presidential address to the RGS in 1920, called *Natural Beauty and Geographical Science*, Younghusband described how he saw mysticism as a means of insight into the material world; his premise being that there are higher states of consciousness to be achieved by mankind but that most people experience ecstasy through sexual union in marriage. This was a theme which he expanded and summed up in his 1942 book *Wedding*.

Younghusband went on to write several more books detailing his further thoughts, how he saw life as an exploration, and to promote ideals of family, team spirit, struggle, ecstasy, and leadership. In contradiction to much of this, he virtually abandoned his wife after he met the woman who would become his young mistress in 1939 and with whom he wrote the book *Wedding*.

He continued to the end to be fascinated by the Himalayas of his early experience and promoted expeditions to Mount Everest through the RGS and The Alpine Club because he especially saw climbing difficult mountains as knitting the perfect unity between body, mind and spirit.

On 20 July 1942, at the World Congress of Faiths in Birmingham, he started his final illness, which ended at his mistress's house in Dorset on 31 July 1942. Younghusband is buried nearby, leaving behind his collected ideas that mysticism, exploration and imperialism were ideally a connected unity.

Chapter 14

Colonel Percy Harrison Fawcett (1867–1925) and, in his wake, (Robert) Peter Fleming OBE (1907–1971)

'We tasted that fierce and irresponsible delight that comes when you are contending with odds to the limits of your physical energies.'
From *A Brazilian Adventure* by Peter Fleming

PERCY HARRISON Fawcett was born on 31 August 1867 at Torquay, Devon, the son of Edward Boyd Fawcett and his wife Myra Elizabeth. In 1925 he disappeared, with one of his sons (Jack) and his son's friend, in the interior of Brazil, while searching for the supposed Lost City of 'Z'. Neither their fate nor their remains were ever discovered and it has even been surmised that they were possibly eaten by cannibals.

After a conventional schooling, Fawcett became a rather earnest and abstemious cadet at Woolwich. He was eventually commissioned into the Royal Artillery and sent to Trincomalee in Ceylon. Here he met his future wife, Nina Agnes Paterson, the daughter of a judge at Galle.

In the early 1890s he was back in England receiving further military instruction followed by a posting to Falmouth. He married in 1901.

Fawcett was sent under cover to Morocco to gather intelligence about the terrain for transport purposes and produced a report. Next, he trained as a land surveyor and received further training in international frontier boundary surveying. He spent some time posted in Hong Kong and then in Colombo, Ceylon, where his first son, Jack, was born in 1903.

After that, Fawcett was posted to County Cork in Ireland and was eventually asked in 1906 to be appointed as chief boundary commissioner for the state of Bolivia. Bolivia had sold a tract of land to Brazil and the boundary was defined on paper as following the courses of two rivers but the courses were not known.

The area was rich in rubber and minerals and it became economically important to know where the boundary was. This was all around the time of the rush for rubber trees or 'rubber madness', begun by Henry Wickham who had smuggled seventy thousand rubber tree seeds out of Brazil and sent them to Kew Gardens– from where they were later spread around Britain's oriental Empire.

Fawcett's specific briefing over the course of three years was to survey the Rio Madeira to the source of the Rio Acre and then follow down the Río Abuná. The dangers were jungle creatures (snakes, pumas, alligators, mosquitoes, piranhas), as well as hostile and aggressive natives. However, he accepted the task with alacrity and set sail for Peru, from there making his way to the Bolivian capital, La Paz. His second son, Brian, was born in England as he arrived in South America, and it was Brian who would eventually go on to sort his father's papers, journals and letters and publish them with a commentary, as a book called *Exploration Fawcett: Journey to the Lost City of Z.*

Fawcett and his team trekked to Lake Titicaca and reached Cobija, where he discovered that his official instruments had not arrived and so he had to use his own. On Boxing Day they left Cobija and went up the Rio Acre to Riberalta. Well within the estimated time scale, by October 1907 Fawcett was able to make his report on his findings to the government in La Paz. They were so pleased that they commissioned him again; this time to survey Bolivia's frontier with Brazil along the Rio Paraguay.

First, Fawcett took home leave to Devon and, then fully and properly equipped, he sailed to Buenos Aires. He and his new team took a steamer to Asunción to begin the survey at Corumbá. The Rio Verde was the border and, exploring it, he found the fascinating flat-topped Ricardo Franco hills. It turned out, according to Fawcett's survey, that Bolivia gained an extra twelve-hundred square miles, over and above the territory that it had previously been believed to have had.

Fawcett was then further asked to survey the Bolivia-Peru border up the unknown Rio Heath. He resigned his army commission and left La Paz with a team in 1911, crossing the Aricona Pass to the Rio Heath. On this trip he saw Inca remains which interested him greatly. In December he submitted his report, resigned his post and went home.

By the end of 1912, myths of great monuments, lost cities and their treasure, as well as hidden tribes, became Percy Fawcett's 'quest'. Back in Bolivia, while surveying land for a mining syndicate, he heard that the First World War had broken out and returned to England. He re-joined the army and saw the War through in France, from January 1915 until 1919 when, again, and promoted to Lieutenant-Colonel, he went home.

Fawcett decided at this point that the family should emigrate to South

America and took them to Jamaica, before himself going back to Brazil. In the national library in Rio de Janeiro, he found an account of a large, hidden and abandoned city which had first been discovered, (in modern times), in 1753. Amazingly, the Brazilian government agreed to fund the cost of an expedition to find this city again. In August 1920 he went to Cuiabà in Mato Grosso, meaning to be there for eighteen months and returning by river. He made for Corumbá and, ultimately, decided to stay there until February 1921.

He took a team into the interior a few times and then went further in on his own, returning with general declarations that he had seen enough to justify further exploration.

Percy was sometimes derided as 'Fawcett the Dreamer' but it is only fair to point out that, among his several real accomplishments, he was a successful army officer and engineer. He had had drawings accepted by the Royal Academy, played cricket for his county, built two racing yachts by himself and took out a patent on the 'Icthoid Curve', a device to add speed to sea-going cutters. Besides all that, he had taken part in the formal delimitation of certain economically important frontiers in South America, as described above. Therefore, there is absolutely no reason to suppose that Percy was less than sincere in his belief that the 'Lost City of Z' really did exist.

Fawcett's family had tired of Jamaica and returned to Devon, and so he went back there too in 1921. He became interested in mysticism and the occult and also applied to the RGS for funding for another expedition. He intended that the party should comprise himself, his elder son, Jack, and his son's friend (neither of whom had experience of difficult exploration in uncharted territory).

In 1924 Fawcett did manage to obtain funds from the *National Geographic* in New York and from a newspaper contract. The team set out from New York for Rio de Janeiro in February 1925 and followed the trail to Cuiabà, where they provisioned themselves and obtained horses and mules and set out to find 'Z'. From this time, they sent correspondence and photographs home, but the last letter was dated 29 May 1925 from the inauspiciously named 'Dead Horse Camp' after one of Fawcett's horses that had died there on an earlier expedition. At this time they were on their own without guides.

Then they simply disappeared, altogether and for ever; probably giving Evelyn Waugh his inspiration for the doom of Tony Last, lost in the Brazilian jungle, in his novel *A Handful of Dust*.

Fawcett's son, Brian, was employed in Peru and so was able to take up the lines of inquiry that arose and even meet an old man in Minas Gerais who claimed to be Percy Fawcett. But Brian was not impressed and did not pursue the matter, despite his mother's wishes.

A search party in 1928 found a uniform case that turned out to have been abandoned by Fawcett years before his final expedition.

Kalapalo Indians also claimed to have helped an older man with two lame, younger, men to travel on eastwards and had noticed them for some days more by the smoke from their fires. An expedition in 1930 to follow this up also disappeared without trace.

In 1932, Peter Fleming OBE (Military Division), (1907–1971), traveller and writer (who was the brother of James Bond creator Ian Fleming and half-brother of famed cellist Amaryllis Fleming), was working at *The Spectator*. He was intrigued by this advertisement in *The Times*:

'Exploring and sporting expedition, under experienced guidance, leaving England June, to explore rivers central Brazil, if possible ascertaining fate of Colonel Fawcett; abundance game, big and small; exceptional fishing; room TWO MORE GUNS; highest references expected and given. Write Box XXX, *The Times*, EC4.'

The results of his successful application to join the expedition are humorously related in his classic travel book *A Brazilian Adventure*, in which, with bathos and wit, he describes the consequential expedition–doomed to failure, owing to delays, procrastination, lack of effective leadership and circumstance as well as clash of personalities, but not *fatally* doomed, as Fawcett's expedition had been. The book has overall been rightly described as similar to something which might have been written by P. G. Wodehouse, at large in the jungle!

Fleming formed the view that Fawcett, a hardened campaigner, soldier and explorer, was actually much better fitted to the expedition than the two younger men and that they had probably fallen behind and then fallen ill. This had kept him from seeking help and they had eventually all perished as a result. Of course, the theory of some that they had all been eaten by cannibals might account for the absence even of bones! Peter Fleming went on to write other travel books, the most famous being the combined *Travels in Tartary*, in which he most entertainingly recounts long treks across Asia.

A 'death bed confession' by a Kalapalo chief who claimed to have murdered all the Fawcett party, produced a skeleton which he said was Fawcett's, but it did not match Fawcett's dental records.

Trace of neither Fawcett nor of his lost city 'Z' has ever been found and the existence of the city seems, ultimately, to have been a myth, after all. There are some limestone hills which, from a distance, might give the impression of a lost city, but that is all.

As Percy's younger son, Brian, says in *Exploration Fawcett: A Journey to The Lost City of Z*, which is an account of the motivation and events leading up to his father's last expedition:

> 'Would that the record of his final, ill-fated trip had come to light! It may yet be found – who knows?'

Who, indeed!

Chapter 15

Gertrude Margaret Lowthian Bell CBE
(1868–1926)

My weary heart eternal silence keeps--
I know not who has slipped into my heart;
Though I am silent, one within me weeps.
My soul shall rend the painted veil apart.
From Gertrude Bell's translation of the poems of Hafiz

BEARING IN mind the recent modern history of Iraq, it is strange indeed to realise that it was a well-educated industrialist's daughter from the north of England who would become responsible for establishing the Iraqi regime that remained in place between the end of the First World War and 1958.

Gertrude Margaret Lowthian Bell was born at Washington Hall, in what was then County Durham (and is now part of Sunderland), on 14 July 1868, the first child and only daughter of Thomas Hugh Bell, industrialist (and later second baronet), by his first wife, Maria (née Shield).

Brought up in the wealth and privilege of the new industrialist class, she received a liberal childhood and education but her early years were blighted by the death of her mother in bearing her brother in 1871. The loss also taught Gertrude a useful measure of self-reliance but was filled to some extent by her father's second marriage in 1876.

Gertrude was the head of the gang of five children that were eventually produced and excelled in intellectual and sporting activities.

She was educated at Queen's College, London W1, (a school for girls), and went up to the relatively new ladies' college, Lady Margaret Hall, Oxford, in April 1886. She possessed fully rounded accomplishments in the intellectual and athletic spheres. In 1888 she was awarded a first-class honours degree in modern history (one of the few degrees that women could take at that time).

After Oxford, Gertrude was sent by her family on a European tour, after the aristocratic template, dating from the eighteenth century. In Romania she met Valentine Chirol, *The Times* correspondent in Eastern Europe, who gave her insights into diplomacy in the modern world. He also introduced her to Charles Hardinge who, later as Viceroy to India, enabled Gertrude to play important roles in the post-First World War Middle East.

She returned to England in late 1889 and divided her time over the next three years between the family home in Redcar and the London summer social season. Gertrude was slim with a fine-boned face, sharp, green eyes, and light-auburn hair. She soon developed a passion for smoking and clothes. However, despite her qualities and the exposure to the season, she did not attract an offer of marriage.

In 1892 she made a visit to Persia, where her stepmother's brother-in-law, Sir Frank Lascelles, was British Minister. She met and fell in love with the embassy's First Secretary, Henry Cadogan, grandson of the third Earl Cadogan. They wished to marry but Gertrude's parents blocked the alliance on the basis that Cadogan had no money and a reputation as a gambler. His death shortly afterwards distressed Gertrude greatly and she started to regard Western Civilisation as providing a harsh environment, in comparison with that of the East.

Back in England she published travel sketches based on her letters, entitled *Safar Nameh: Persian Pictures*, which praised Persia and the Persian civilisation. Then, having learned Persian with Sandford Strong, she made a free verse translation of the mystical poet Hafiz which was published as *Poems from the Divan of Hafiz* and received critical acclaim.

During the 1890s Gertrude travelled a great deal with family and friends in France, Germany, Italy, and Switzerland. She even undertook a world tour by ocean liner with her brother, Maurice.

In the summers between 1899–1904, she undertook a series of arduous expeditions in the Alps, culminating in the ascent of the Matterhorn in August 1904.

Gertrude visited Jerusalem early in 1900 and journeyed on horseback to Petra, Palmyra, (in the footsteps of *The Queen of The Desert*), and Baalbek, which gave her an interest in Syrian archaeology.

Back in Jerusalem in January 1905, she went through the Syrian desert to Konia in Asia Minor and then published *The Desert and the Sown* which became a contemporary classic of travel writing. The 'sown' areas were the towns dominated by the Turks, whereas the desert areas were dominated by the Bedouin tribes. By now, Gertrude was finding travel in the Middle East to be an escape from the suffocating constraints of home life.

In December 1906 she set out to resume the architectural and archaeological researches she had already begun in Anatolia. She met up with archaeologist Sir William Ramsay in May 1907 and they explored the Hittite and Byzantine site of Bin-Bir-Kilisse in Turkey.

Gertrude compiled a chronology of Byzantine churches in their study and they then published their findings in *The Thousand and One Churches*.

In 1909 she surveyed the Roman and Byzantine fortresses on the banks of the Euphrates in Mesopotamia, detailing an account of her efforts in *Amurath to Amurath* in which she also tried to raise the profile of the Young Turks' liberating movement to the benefit of Muslim and non-Muslim alike.

In 1911 she was back in Mesopotamia undertaking a fuller survey of the palace of Al-Ukhaidir which remains one of the best surviving examples of early Islamic architecture. Gertrude's findings were initially published in the *Hellenic Journal* and then the masterly *The Palace and Mosque of Ukhaidir: a Study in Early Mohammadan Architecture*. She also surveyed and photographed early Christian architecture in Mesopotamia (some of which buildings have since been destroyed).

Gertrude's spells in England between her expeditions were partly spent in becoming a founder member and later president of the northern section of the Women's National Anti-Suffrage League, (begun in 1908 and chaired by Lady Jersey), which merged with the National League for Opposing Woman Suffrage. Gertrude also supported Mary Ward's Local Government Advancement Committee, founded in 1912, to promote the idea of an increase in women's public service in local government, where (they claimed), their knowledge and experience most suited them to serve.

Gertrude first met Charles Hotham Montagu Doughty-Wylie in 1907 in Konia, when he was serving as British military vice-consul. He was a married army officer but they fell in love. Despite her family's rather stiff-as-a-poker attitudes, he even visited Gertrude's family home at Rounton in 1913. However, the affair never proceeded beyond correspondence, and his death at Gallipoli in 1915 (leading a victorious charge, armed only with a cane, for which he received a posthumous Victoria Cross), caused her deep grief.

Between 1913–14, Gertrude went to Ha'il in central Arabia, the seat of the Banu Rashid dynasty. Her aim was to take up the challenge of the desert and to understand the people who dwelt in it, especially their rulers. In 1913 she was elected as one of the first women fellows of the RGS. For the expedition, she set out from Damascus with her caravan in December 1913. They crossed the Nefud desert, and reached Ha'il in February 1914. In the absence of Emir Ibn Rashid, she was held captive there for eleven days and, presumably, learned something of desert people from this. Gertrude received the RGS's gold medal for her expedition in 1918.

At the beginning of the First World War, Gertrude served as an officer of the Red Cross searching for missing and wounded soldiers before she was recalled in February 1915 to reorganise the headquarters in London.

In the autumn of 1915, the military intelligence department in Cairo needed the expertise of British subjects with knowledge of pre-war Arabia. Gertrude was well qualified and she reached Cairo at the end of November 1915. The organisation soon became called The Arab Bureau to deal with Britain's policy in the Arab region. T. E. Lawrence-of-Arabia was one of the others also engaged in the Bureau. The objective was to rid Arabia of the Turks and to provide Britain with grateful Arabs who would favour Britain's interests after the war.

In 1916 Gertrude was commissioned by the Indian Viceroy, Lord Hardinge, to go Basrah on a liaison mission as the Viceroy's envoy in order to assess the probable conflicts of intention between the Arab Bureau's schemes and the schemes of the India Office. The conflict had arisen from the Arab Bureau's willingness to encourage Arab nationalism as a tool in the overall objective, whereas the India Office wished to aim for more direct British control.

Gertrude was stationed at the headquarters of the Mesopotamian Expeditionary Force and part of her job was to gather information on the movements of Bedouin tribes in central Arabia and in the Sinai peninsula.

In Basrah, in June 1916, she joined the staff of Sir Percy Cox, who was the chief political officer with the expeditionary force. Gertrude was appointed assistant political officer.

Baghdad was captured from the Turks by Lieutenant-General Sir Stanley Maude in March 1917, and Gertrude continued as Cox's assistant in the administration of Mesopotamia. In 1917 she was admitted to the order of Commander of the British Empire for her services and also served under his successor, Lieutenant-Colonel Arnold Wilson.

Gertrude became convinced of the viability of Arab self-government with British advisers. This was at odds with Wilson's belief in direct British rule. Gertrude completed *A Review of the Civil Administration of Mesopotamia* which was published as a Parliamentary White Paper in 1920.

The San Remo conference in April 1920 gave Britain the League of Nations' mandate over Iraq but tribal disturbances (with a range of causes) erupted which resulted in the establishment of a provisional Arab government under the Naqib of Baghdad. Cox returned as British High Commissioner and appointed Gertrude as his oriental secretary.

At the Cairo Conference in March 1921, Winston Churchill, as Colonial Secretary, accepted the position of Cox and Gertrude that Britain should keep a presence in Iraq by the use of British advisers on loan to the Arab government. Feisal ibn Hussein ascended the throne and Gertrude attracted the title *Khatun* ('Lady of the Court'). She was also instrumental in the ratification of the Anglo-Iraqi Treaty of 1922 which replaced the mandate from the League of Nations.

Gertrude then became involved in organising the first elections for a democratic assembly and supervising the constitutional reforms needed to give legitimacy to the new regime. She was also involved in settling the frontiers of Iraq with Jordan, Saudi Arabia and Turkey, as well as trying to liberate the Muslim women who were generally confined to their homes in Baghdad.

Gertrude's influence in Iraq lessened in 1924 when a new constitution was established. Moreover, she fell in love again; this time with Kinahan Cornwallis, personal adviser to the King, but he did not respond to her and so she turned her energies back to archaeology and started a Museum in Baghdad.

Gertrude took sick leave in England in the summer of 1925. On her return to Iraq, she died in her sleep at Baghdad during the night of 11–12 July 1926; the cause being an overdose of sleeping tablets. She was buried on the evening of the 12 July in the British military cemetery at Baghdad and a memorial service was later held at St Margaret's, Westminster. Whatever her friends might have thought, there was no sufficient evidence of suicide which, of course, at that time, was a criminal offence. There is a window dedicated to her memory in St Lawrence's Church, East Rounton, North Yorkshire.

Her friend Janet Courtney summed Gertrude Bell up with these words: 'With a man's grasp of affairs, she united a woman's quick instinct.'

Writing in the *Geographical Journal* D. G. Hogarth said very charmingly of her:

'No woman in recent time has combined her qualities – her taste for arduous and dangerous adventure with her scientific interest and knowledge, her competence in archaeology and art, her distinguished literary gift, her sympathy for all sorts and condition of men, her political insight and appreciation of human values, her masculine vigour, hard common sense and practical efficiency – all tempered by feminine charm and a most romantic spirit.'

Chapter 16

George Herbert Leigh Mallory (1886–1924)

New York Times reporter: 'Why climb Everest?'
George Mallory: 'Because it's there.'

GEORGE HERBERT Leigh Mallory was born on 18 June 1886 at Mobberley, Cheshire, the eldest son of Herbert Leigh Mallory, rector of Mobberley, and his wife, Annie (née Beridge Jebb). He was educated under a scholarship at Winchester College.

Mallory and other pupils were taken climbing in the Alps by R.L.G. Irving, one of Mallory's school masters at Winchester. In 1905 he went up to Magdalene College, Cambridge, where he became something of a socialist and joined the Fabian Society and the Marlowe Dramatic Club, falling in with the 'Bloomsbury Group' along the way. He also captained the Magdalene College boat.

As is often the case with students who split their time between academic study and sporting and social activities, Mallory was awarded a second-class degree in history and then wrote an essay which he later published as *Boswell the Biographer*.

After this and between 1909–1910, he stayed for five months at Roquebrune in the Alpes Maritimes to prepare himself to teach French.

Around this time he went mountaineering in the Alps, around the Cumberland Lakes and in North Wales, but he did not often write about his experiences, believing climbing to be a living art in its own right. He had a mixed reputation as a rock-climber for although he was noted for his essential skill he was also reckless, obstinate and obstreperous with climbing partners.

In 1910 Mallory took a post as an assistant school master at Charterhouse, in Godalming, where he taught English, history, and French. He also introduced some of his pupils to mountaineering.

On 29 July 1914 Mallory married Christiana Ruth, daughter of Hugh Thackeray Turner, an architect. They had a son and two daughters. As he was in a 'reserved occupation' he could not join up in the forces when war was declared in 1914. He was, though, later commissioned in the Royal Garrison Artillery as 2nd Lieutenant in December 1915, and took part in the Battle of the Somme.

He served as a liaison officer with the French and was promoted to First Lieutenant before he was invalided home.

Mallory joined the first Everest expedition in 1921 under the influence of Geoffrey Young. In the same year, he explored the Tibetan side of Mount Everest and reached the North Col with Guy Henry Bullock and several porters. They had noticed a valley on the Nepali side of Everest that Mallory called 'The Western Cwm'.

The following year Mallory returned to Everest and reached a height of 26,902ft without bottled oxygen. During the descent he saved the lives of three companions when they slipped and fell.

After Australian George Finch's expedition went even higher (to 27,300ft with extra oxygen), and noting Finch's high speed of ascent, Mallory decided to make an attempt to reach the North Col after a heavy snowstorm. He failed, and an avalanche killed several porters, for which Mallory attracted adverse criticism.

After this, he lectured on climbing Everest in Britain and in America. In March 1923 it was reported by the *New York Times* that, when Mallory was asked, 'Why climb Everest?' he replied, 'Because it's there.'

In May 1923, Mallory became a lecturer and assistant secretary on the Cambridge University board of extra-mural studies. In 1924 he was unexpectedly promoted to climbing leader on the intended next Everest expedition (funded by the RGS), when Colonel E. F. Norton replaced General C. G. Bruce, as superintendent. It has come to light in research carried out by Jeffrey Archer in writing his book about Mallory, called *Paths of Glory*, that Mallory had wanted George Finch (with whom he had climbed several times) to be his climbing partner but that the RGS baulked at the idea of an Australian on the expedition (to share the glory) and blocked the request. Mallory then refused to go without him until the Prince of Wales appealed to his 'patriotism' and asked him not to take Finch. That is how Andrew Comyn Irvine (b. 1902) was eventually chosen, an inexperienced second choice, to accompany Mallory on his fatal expedition. Finch's greater strength and experience might well have contributed to a happier result.

Now, on to a point of detail. Although Mallory was in principle opposed to the use of bottled oxygen, he recalled Finch's success with it in 1922, and changed his mind.

Mallory seems to have become obsessed with climbing to the summit. The final plan was that he and Irvine would make the final ascent with oxygen. Mallory told Ruth: 'It is almost unthinkable with this plan that I shan't get to the top. I can't see myself coming down defeated'. In the end he did not come down at all.

For the final push, Mallory and Irvine left their camp on the north-east ridge on 8 June 1924 and were allegedly spotted through a break in the clouds by Noel Odell, at 12.50 hours. He said they were probably on a rock outcrop known as the 'Second Step' below the final summit pyramid. However, given that Odell only had a glimpse, during a short break in cloud cover, their exact, final position when last seen is uncertain.

Mallory and Irvine then disappeared and, assuming that they had perished, the expedition erected a memorial cairn at the foot of the mountain. Memorial services were held at various locations, including St Paul's Cathedral. Among several memorials, there is a court named for George Mallory in Magdalene College, Cambridge.

No one knows, despite all the speculation, whether Mallory and Irvine did conquer the ascent of Everest. As Edmund Hillary said later (and Mallory's son John agreed), mountaineering is not just about climbing mountains successfully, it is also about descending them successfully and this Mallory and Irvine did not achieve.

Jeffrey Archer suggests in his book that the absence of the photograph of Ruth from Mallory's wallet (where he always kept it), suggests that he left it at the summit. Mallory's daughter supported the claim on the basis that Mallory had said that he would leave the picture at the summit. However, in the absence of any other evidence, it seems a tenuous suggestion, and it would surely make more sense had Mallory made a note on the back of it, recording a full ascent, and kept it in his wallet 'just in case'. One other suggestion is that Mallory's snow goggles were in his pocket when his body was found; this might indicate that, when he fell he was not wearing them because it was dark, and he would not be climbing up in the dark – but down. However, this presupposes that they had already got to the top and leaves out altogether the fact that he might have lost the goggles he was wearing when he fell; falling being consistent with a rope burn found around his waist.

In 1933 an ice axe which, from markings, might have been Irvine's, was found on rocks below the First Step. In 1975 a Chinese climber found 'a dead English'. An expedition in 1999 found Mallory's body (identified by a name tag in the clothing), and he was reburied in the snow on the mountain that had claimed him. Apart from the ice axe, no trace of Irvine has ever been found.

However, a George Mallory *has* been up to the top of Everest. On 14 May 1995, George Mallory's grandson went there, later commenting that he had been 'commemorating the successful completion of a little outstanding family business.'

The mystery, though, remains. Veteran mountaineer Sir Chris Bonington has said that he would like to think that Mallory and Irvine had made it and pointed to the rush that hits climbers when they are near a summit. That, combined with Mallory's self-belief and utter determination to get there, are powerful pointers to the fact that Mallory and Irvine *might* have ascended to the summit of Mount Everest. However, given that they are still up there, it cannot quite be said, in any event, that they had *conquered* the mountain.

Chapter 17

Dame Freya Madeline Stark DBE
(ca. 1893–1993)

An Imaginative aunt who, for my ninth birthday, sent a copy of the Arabian Nights was, I suppose, the original cause of trouble.

Unfostered and unnourished, the little flame so kindled fed secretly on dreams. Chance, such as the existence of a Syrian missionary near my home, nourished it, and Fate, with long months of illness and leisure, blew it to a blaze bright enough to light my way through labyrinths of Arabic, and eventually to land me on the coast of Syria at the end of 1927.

From *The Valleys of the Assassins* by Freya Stark

FREYA MADELINE Stark is believed to have been born in a studio on Rue Denfert Rochereau, Paris, on 31 January 1893, but the exact date and place are uncertain. She was the elder daughter of Robert Stark (a sculptor), and his wife, Flora Madeline (a painter and pianist), who had one further daughter, called Vera, born in Italy ca. 1895. Freya was used to travel from an early age; between France, Devon (where the mother and daughters normally resided and where her father came to renovate property), and Italy. In 1903 Freya's mother and the girls settled at Dronero, in Italy, and her father stayed in Devon until he emigrated to Canada in 1911, leaving Freya bereft and constantly seeking father-figures throughout her life.

At Dronero her mother invested in, and managed, a silk factory (Freya's sister would later marry the owner), and it was there that Freya suffered traumatic disfigurement as a child when her hair and even her eyelids were caught in the machinery. The overall effect of this, corrective skin grafting, and the long convalescence, plainly had a lasting impact on the girl who started a lifelong habit of suddenly taking to her bed.

Freya was educated at home and then read history at Bedford College, London, where she met William Paton Ker, a professor of English, who took her mountaineering in the Alps in 1913, and from this, she gained an enduring interest in mountains and mountaineering.

During the First World War she trained in nursing at Bologna, and nearly married an Italian doctor. She also went on a walking tour of Europe with her friend Venetia Buddicom and, in 1924 became only the second woman to climb the east face of Monte Rosa.

During a period of convalescence from one of her many illnesses and indispositions, Freya took Arabic lessons with a view to becoming a governess in the Middle East. She also read Arabic for a time at the School of Oriental Studies in London.

In 1926, her parents' friend, Herbert Young, offered to leave his Asolo house to Freya if she would live in it. Freya moved with her mother to Young's house, which became known locally as 'Casa Freia'.

In 1927 Freya lived in the Lebanon for some months and then journeyed through Syria with her friend Buddicom. In 1929 she moved to Baghdad, then under British influence, where, after the manner of Sir Richard Burton (and scandalising the stuffed-shirt brigade), she went amongst the people in Arab disguise to glean information. Also, rather after the fashion of Hester Stanhope and Jane Digby, she was accorded recognition by the Arabs as a great female adventurer after her extraordinary trips to Lurestan and the Alamut District of Mazandaran. The War Office was able to make maps from her surveys.

Freya worked for a time as a journalist in Baghdad and fell in love with a Captain Holt who was a diplomat but he did not respond to her. He did, though, give her briefings about the Kurdistan uprising, which she published in *The Times*. Freya then inherited her father's money in 1931 and this brought her increased freedom.

In 1933 Freya was awarded the Back Grant from the RGS and was the first woman to receive the Burton Medal of the Royal Asiatic Society (named for Sir Richard Burton). She wrote and published *The Valleys of the Assassins* in 1934 and this was a great success. It still remains in print, along with most of her twenty-three other travel books.

In 1935 she went to Hadhramaut, southern Arabia, in search of an ancient trade route to such places as Timna in Qataban. After she succumbed to one of her periodic illnesses there, the Royal Air Force flew her to a hospital in Aden.

Freya was now internationally noted as a traveller and adventurer and, for her book *The Southern Gates of Arabia* (1936), she received the Mungo Park Medal from the Royal Scottish Geographical Society.

Between 1937 and 1938, she returned to Arabia with the archaeologist

Gertrude Caton-Thompson on an expedition sponsored by the RGS, but taking to her bed in a characteristic fit of sulky hypochondria, fell out with the rest of the party and then returned, on a camel, over the desert, on her own.

During the Second World War Freya was a member of the Ministry of Information as an expert on southern Arabia, and was posted to Aden, Yemen, and Egypt. In Egypt she became friends with General Wavell and founded, as a propaganda initiative, what she called the 'Brotherhood of Freedom', which promoted the democratic ideal, countered fascism and fostered British support through the unlikely (but very British) medium of secret tea parties! By 1941 she was back in Baghdad trying to introduce her notions in Iraq. In 1943 Wavell was first promoted to Field Marshal and then appointed Viceroy of India and he invited Freya to India. Wavell lent her a government car for the return journey to Tehran but on arrival, she sold the car and kept the proceeds of sale which caused a stir but nothing seems to have been done about it.

As an unquestioning supporter of the British Empire, Freya lectured on Palestine in the United States between 1943–4 to try to stop the spread of anti-British opinion by the Zionist movement.

After the war she returned to Italy and started establishing English reading rooms, as well as publishing a collection of essays, called *Perseus in the Wind* (1948), and the first part of her autobiography, *Traveller's Prelude* (1950). For some reason she married Stewart Henry Perowne, a former diplomatic colleague at Aden, Cairo, and Baghdad, in October 1947, in London. Presumably Freya knew that he was homosexual but could not have fully understood the implications and they finally separated in 1952.

She wrote the rest of her autobiography in *Beyond the Euphrates* (1951), *The Coast of Incense* (1953) and *Dust in the Lion's Paw* (1961), and between 1974 and 1982 she published eight volumes of her letters.

In *Ionia: A Quest* (1954) Freya visited places described by Herodotus in Asia Minor. She also published other books in a similar vein and still travelled adventurously, even going to Afghanistan in 1968 and to Nepal in 1970. She received the founder's medal from the RGS, the Percy Sykes memorial medal from the Royal Central Asiatic Society, and honorary doctorates from Glasgow and Durham universities. She was appointed Commander of the British Empire in 1953 and advanced to Dame of the British Empire in 1972. Freya had been made a sister in the Order of St John of Jerusalem in 1949 and was advanced to a sister commander in 1981. In a nice Italian tribute, she was given the keys of Asolo in 1984.

Few were indifferent to Freya Stark. People whom she met either loved her or disliked her intensely but she had many friends and an easy social manner (imparted by her mother), which helped her in her many travels.

Freya lived to be 100 but she was senile for the last five years and died on 9 May 1993 in Asolo where she is buried in the cemetery. *The Times* called her 'The last of the Romantic Travellers' and *The New York Times* related her reaction to being asked about death when she was ninety-three years old: 'I feel about it as about the first ball, or the first meet of hounds, anxious as to whether one will get it right, and timid and inexperienced – all the feelings of youth'. The newspaper also referred to her writing as demonstrating 'spirit, authority and humour' and summed her up with the words: 'She was the consummate traveller because of her fearlessness, candour, charm, idealism and a streak of näiveté.'

Chapter 18

Sir Francis Charles Chichester KBE
(1901–1972)

Asked why he had made his solo circumnavigation, Francis Chichester replied, 'Because it intensifies life'.

FRANCIS CHARLES Chichester was an aviator as well as a sailor but his greatest skill in both was as a navigator. He was born on 17 September 1901, at Shirwell, Devon, the younger son of Charles Chichester (a younger son of a baronet), vicar of Shirwell, and his wife, Emily Annie (née Page). He was educated at the infants' school in Barnstaple, at preparatory schools in Ellerslie and Bournemouth, and then at Marlborough College, where he was unhappy and left at the age of seventeen.

Chichester emigrated to New Zealand in December 1919 with only ten pounds in his pocket. He tried a variety of jobs until as an estate agent and property developer, he was able to earn a comfortable income. He married Muriel Eileen (née Blakiston) in 1923 and they had one son who survived childhood but died in 1967. They soon separated and Muriel died in 1929. Their son was brought up by his maternal grandparents until Chichester married again.

Between August 1966 and 28 May 1967, he became the first person to sail on his own (a distance of 29,600 miles) around the world in 226 days. I remember as a seven year old being taken to Plymouth Hoe to watch him enter the port to a tumultuous welcome of around 250,000 people, some of whom, in little boats, escorted him over the finishing line at 20:58 hours. He was greeted by the Lord Mayor of Plymouth, to sounding sirens and a ten-gun salute from the Royal Artillery. Having already been awarded a knighthood on arrival in Australia, he was dubbed with Sir Francis Drake's sword by the Queen in an open-air ceremony at Greenwich, and the Post Office even issued a stamp to commemorate his feat.

Asked what he most wanted once he was ashore, he said: 'What I would like, after four months of my own cooking, is the best dinner, from the best chef, in the best surroundings, in the best company.'

The Sir Francis Chichester Trust is an outward bound organisation which was established in his memory. The *Gipsy Moth IV* is on permanent display in dry dock at Greenwich, near the recently restored *Cutty Sark*, and Chichester wrote a book about the voyage, called *Gipsy Moth Circles the World*.

The idea for the voyage had developed over the years since Chichester had been a record-breaker in small aircraft, largely owing to his extraordinary ability as a navigator.

He had formed an aviation company and learned to fly at a New Zealand air force base. He returned to England after ten years and took further flying lessons at Brooklands, bought a de Havilland Gipsy I Moth, obtained his 'A' licence, and made a flying tour of Europe.

In 1929 Chichester set off to fly to Australia. After a nineteen-day solo flight and a variety of incidents and accidents, he landed at Sydney, New South Wales, to a tremendous welcome from thousands of people. He was only the second pilot (after Australian Bert Hinkler in 1928) to successfully accomplish this dangerous operation.

In New Zealand, Chichester decided to make the first solo flight from east to west across the Tasman Sea. This meant that he would have to land to refuel on two small islands, roughly equally spaced across the ocean. This required the exercise of perfect skills of navigation. He had fitted floats to his *Gipsy I Moth* to enable him to land on the island lagoons. He made landings at Norfolk Island, and Lord Howe Island where his plane sank and had to be rebuilt, before he reached Jarvis Bay, south of Sydney. He decided to continue a round the world tour but crashed in Japan, injuring himself and writing off his plane.

After returning to England once more, Chichester married Sheila Mary Craven in 1937 and they had one son. They lived for a year in New Zealand and then decided to settle in England. Chichester then took a job as a navigation specialist with a firm of instrument makers.

During the Second World War, Chichester was eventually appointed navigation officer at the Empire Flying School (1943–5). After the war he established his own business recycling, and then publishing, maps and guide books.

It was only at this time that he took up yacht racing; at first as the navigator and, from 1958, solo with his own boat, *Gipsy Moth II*.

In the late 1950s Chichester contracted what was diagnosed at the time as lung cancer but recovered from the illness and in 1960, with *Gipsy Moth*

II, won the first solo transatlantic race. In the same race two years later he shaved nearly seven days off his previous record but even so, only came second.

Gipsy Moth IV was built for him to sail around the world which, as we know, he achieved, having made just one stop-over at Sydney.

He later failed in his attempt, in *Gipsy Moth V*, to sail 4,000 miles in twenty days, from Guinea Bissau across the Atlantic to Nicaragua, but his time of twenty-two days did establish another record.

Chichester had to turn back from the 1972 solo transatlantic race, owing to failing health. He died on 26 August 1972, at Plymouth – scene of his greatest triumph – and was buried at Shirwell.

Chapter 19

Amy Johnson CBE (1903–1941)

There's a little lady, who has captured every heart,
Amy Johnson, it's you…
I'm proud of the way you flew,
Believe me, Amy
You cannot blame me, Amy, for falling in love with you.
From Wonderful Amy, lyrics by Joseph George Gilbert,
music by Lawrence Wright (as Horatio Nicholls).

AMY JOHNSON was born on 1 July 1903 in Kingston-upon-Hull, Yorkshire, to John William Johnson, a merchant, and his wife, Amy (née Hodge). She graduated from Sheffield University with a BA in Economics in 1925 and then worked in a London solicitor's office.

Obsessed with the thought of flying, fed up with office work and told by her employer to choose between the office and flying, Amy chose flying. By now she was an attractive young woman, 5ft 4in tall, with blue eyes and light-brown hair. Amy joined the technical school of the De Havilland aircraft company at Stag Lane, Edgware, London, (founded on 25 September 1920), and started learning to fly, under the guidance of Captain Valentine 'Bake' Baker MC, AFC, in 1928. On 6 July 1929 she won her pilot's 'A' licence and, on 10 December 1929, was awarded the first licensed ground engineer's licence given by the Air Ministry to a woman. De Havilland saw an advertising opportunity in her: if this little girl could fly and fix their airplanes then it could not be that difficult. At the London Flying Club at Stag Lane, she met the director of civil aviation, Sir Sefton Brancker, and Sir Charles Wakefield of Castrol who, along with the Royal Dutch-Shell Oil Company, decided to realise her desire to try to break the light airplane record in a solo flight to Australia.

On 5 May 1930, Amy Johnson took off from Croydon airfield in her second-hand, two-year-old Gipsy Moth light biplane, *Jason*, to try to break

(Australian) Squadron Leader Bert Hinkler's 1928 London to Australia record of fifteen and a half days. She was ahead of Hinkler's time when she arrived at Karachi on 10 May. She then flew over to Calcutta and had planned to fly non-stop to Rangoon and then on to Singapore but was delayed by bad weather and shortage of fuel.

Finally landing at Darwin, Australia, after nineteen and a half days, Amy was given a tumultuous welcome, which she was unused to dealing with and found rather difficult. The King congratulated her and she was appointed a Commander of the British Empire and awarded the Harmon Trophy. There was even a popular song written about her called *Amy, Wonderful Amy*. After crashing her airplane in Brisbane, her future husband James Mollison, another pilot, flew her on to Sydney.

On her return to England, Amy was met by the Secretary of State for Air. Her airplane from this flight to Australia is in the Science Museum.

Her achievement was the first of many other long-distance flights. On 26 July 1931, accompanied by a mechanic in *Jason II*, she took off for Tokyo over the Soviet Union and arrived on 6 August in seventy-eight hours and fifty minutes. Amy and Mollison married on 29 July 1932. On 14 November 1932 she set out from Lympne, in Kent, for Cape Town by the West African route, and covered the 6,200 miles in her Puss Moth in four days, six hours and forty-five minutes, beating Mollison's previous record by ten hours.

On 22 July 1933 Amy and her husband left Pendine Sands, Carmarthenshire, in a heavily-loaded, ten-seat De Havilland Dragon, *Seafarer*, to fly to New York. After thirty-nine hours they ran out of fuel and were forced to crash land at Bridgeport, Connecticut. Despite failure in the main objective of the flight, they had set a record as the first husband and wife team to cross the Atlantic east-to-west, as well as making the first direct Britain to America flight by 'plane.

By late 1934, Amy's marriage had broken down because of Mollison's heavy drinking and adultery. The Bridgeport crash (for which she blamed him), was the final straw and they separated. Amy eventually divorced Mollison in 1938 and reverted to her maiden name.

Between 1935 and 1937, Amy was President of the Women's Engineering Society.

In 1936 she had failed in her entry in the King's cup race in a new British Aircraft Eagle monoplane. At the same time, her 1930 Australian record was beaten, by four days, by New Zealander Jean Gardner Batten ('the Greta Garbo of the skies').

However, Amy made another flight – to Cape Town, between 4 and 7 May 1936 in a Percival Gull. She arrived in Cape Town in three days, six hours and eleven minutes, and the round trip beat the existing outbound, homebound, and double-flight records.

In 1939 she wrote the book *Skyroads of the World*.

In May 1938 Amy was appointed national leader of the Women's Air Reserve and undertook many training flights. However, it was not until March 1940 that her friend Pauline Gower asked her to join the Air Transport Auxiliary. In this role she shuttled planes back and forth from Hatfield, near the ATA base at White Waltham, to Prestwick.

Amy's last flight was on 5 January 1941, in an ATA Airspeed Oxford, flying from Blackpool to RAF Kidlington. She was warned by flying control about the adverse weather conditions but chose to ignore the warning and took off at 11.45 am in bitterly cold conditions with heavy cloud, snow and fog.

The official version of what happened is that the weather did not clear and she lost her way. Forced to bale out over the perilous Thames Estuary, she was seen alive in the water. They tried to throw her lines from a ship but she could not grasp them. Lieutenant Commander Walter Fletcher RN, of LHM Trawler *Haslemere*, gallantly dived overboard and tried to rescue her but he perished in the attempt and Amy's body was never recovered. Another theory is that her airplane was mistaken for an enemy aircraft and shot down; those responsible being involved in a subsequent cover-up.

On 14 January 1941 a memorial service was held for Amy in St Martin-in-the-Fields.

Amy Johnson was not the greatest aviator who ever lived and certainly not the greatest navigator, but her courage, enthusiasm and recklessness, besides the manner and mystery of her death, have made her name legendary.

Besides her CBE, Amy Johnson's honours included the President's Gold Medal of the Society of Engineers (1931); the Egyptian Gold Medal for Valour (1930); The Women's Trophy of the International League of Aviators (1930); the Segrave Trophy (1933); the Gold Medal of Honour of the League of Youth (1933), and the Gold Medal of the Royal Aero Club (1936). A Women's Engineering Society (WES) scholarship for women in aeronautics was established in her memory in February 1941.

There is a statue (by Harry Ibbetson) of Amy in Kingston-upon-Hull and there are many streets named after her, as well as an engineering building at Sheffield University. The Royal Aeronautical Society hosts an annual lecture in her memory, as near as possible to 6 July, which is the anniversary of the issue of her pilot's licence.

Chapter 20

Gladys May Aylward (1902–1970)

Wherefore by their fruits ye shall know them.

St Matthew 7:20

GLADYS AYLWARD, missionary to China, was just one of many young people who, during the age of Empire and muscular Christianity, evangelised far-flung corners of the earth. But a journalist eventually caught up with her and wrote of her determined exploits which Gladys undertook in the face of all manner of obstacles and dangers and, in a sense, wrote of her as an example for them all.

Alan Burgess wrote a book about her and then they made a stirring film, *The Inn of The Sixth Happiness* (1958), starring Ingrid Bergman (ironically as the very plain, 4ft 10in tall Aylward), Robert Donat (as the local Mandarin) and Curt Jürgens. Ingrid Bergman was divorced and the development of the love interest represented by Curt Jürgens was fictional, so Gladys Aylward refused to have anything to do with the film and even refused to go to see it. Nevertheless, it continues to play on television channels and now has the further poignancy that it was the last film the desperately ill Robert Donat would ever make; his film character fading into the darkness towards the end of the film, as he bade farewell.

Gladys May Aylward was born into humble circumstances in Edmonton, North London, on 24 February 1902 and was brought up by her parents with two siblings, receiving a standard elementary education of the time. At fourteen she was employed in a shop and, after that, became a nanny and then a parlour maid, working in households in the West End of London.

Influenced by her father joining a local gospel mission, in 1929 Aylward was accepted by the China Inland Mission for training to be a missionary but she was found unsuitable and, to her grave disappointment, they declined to let her work for them, telling her that she could never learn Chinese or undertake the work.

The China Inland Mission had been founded on 25 June 1865, when James Hudson Taylor had prayed on the beach at Brighton for 'twenty-four willing, skillful labourers to reach the inland provinces of China.' Once they became established, these inland missionaries adopted (unusually for the times), local customs, food, dress and language in order to spread their message; a pattern that Gladys Aylward would later follow independently.

Undaunted by her rejection by the Mission, she then went to work in the slums of Bristol and Swansea where she fell ill and nearly died. Returning home to her parents at Edmonton, Gladys went to a Primitive Methodist meeting in Wood Green. There she learned that a Mrs Jeannie Lawson, head of an independent mission in north China, needed an assistant but that he or she would have to find their own passage out.

Fired-up by the renewed prospects of an actual engagement as a missionary, Gladys returned to domestic service to earn and save enough money to buy a one-way railway ticket on the Trans-Siberian Railway, which went across the interior of the Soviet Union (during the Russo-Chinese War). Her employment coincidentally included that as parlour maid in the household of the daughter of fellow adventurer Sir Francis Younghusband in South Kensington and, in the film mentioned above, there is the dramatisation of a real event there, when Gladys placed her Bible and saved money on the bed and prayed: 'Oh, God, here's me. Here's my Bible. Here's my money. Use us, God, use us!' – because, according to her simple belief, we are all responsible for each other.

She left Liverpool Street Station on 15 October 1932 with two pounds in her pocket and a suitcase full of food and, after a long, cold and arduous journey (even dodging gunfire from the hostilities between Russia and China), arrived without formal qualifications or commendation, in the town of Yungcheng, in Shanxi Province, where she was relieved to find herself amongst people as short and dark-haired as she was.

She met the missionary, Mrs Jeannie Lawson (a dour Scot), of whom she had heard in Wood Green. Mrs Lawson immediately took her on and they began a project using an inn and its hospitality (including the telling of bible stories to their guests), to spread the word of God.

Gladys lived simply in a small room, with a small bed, two stools, two cups and a basin, and on a wall was displayed a card bearing the words:

'God hath chosen the weak things. I can do all things through Christ who strengthens me.'

She even started an orphanage: one day in the street she came across a beggar who had stolen a sickly girl to help him beg. Gladys paid him ninepence for her and 'Ninepence' became her name. After a while, Ninepence came in one day with a little orphan boy and said that she would eat less if he could be taken in too, and so he was named 'Less'. The orphanage, which had begun with one child grew and grew.

On Mrs Lawson's death, Gladys was appointed foot inspector by the local Mandarin to supervise and enforce the banning of female foot binding (by which girls' feet were tightly bound to prevent them growing naturally, just for the sake of having beautiful, small feet). She excelled at this task and used the opportunity to spread the word still further. Her name in Chinese was interpreted as Ai Weh-Te ('Virtuous One') and she became greatly loved by the community which she served.

In 1940, during the Japanese War, Gladys was beaten by Japanese soldiers and, fearing for the children of the area, amidst the fighting led a hundred of them across the Yellow River and the mountains, for twelve days, to safety at Fufeng, where she collapsed from a mixture of exhaustion, malnutrition, pneumonia and typhoid fever. A Colonel Linnan, who had fallen in love with her, visited her in her convalescence and proposed marriage but Gladys refused as it would have prevented her from continuing her work.

Eventually, she recovered, and went to work among lepers. Gladys became a Chinese citizen in 1941.

In 1949 she was able to return to England and although her return to China was, despite her citizenship, blocked by the communist Chinese authorities, in 1958 she decided to undertake speaking tours and travel to Taiwan to continue her vocation. Gladys started another orphanage there in which she worked until she died, aged just under sixty-eight years old.

She was buried on 2 January 1970 in the hilltop garden of Christ's College, Tamsui, beneath a splendid marble monument, inscribed with her details and the words, from St John 12:24:

'Unless a grain of wheat falls into the earth and dies, it remains alone;
but if it dies it bears much fruit.'

Chapter 21

Krystyna Skarbek-Granville GM, OBE, Croix de Guerre, born (ca. 1908–1952)

> Le vent souffle sur les tombes,
> La Liberté
> reviendra.
> On nous oubliera,
> Nous rentrerons dans l'ombre
>
> From *Complainte du Partisan* by
> Emmanuel d'Astier de la Vigerie

KRYSTYNA Skarbek-Granville was a Polish aristocrat who found herself accidentally exiled from Poland on the outbreak of the Second World War. This is a brief account of her life, including her recruitment to the British Special Operations Executive ('SOE') and some of her exploits in it, including the extrication of three senior SOE agents, who had been summarily condemned to death at the hands of the Gestapo.

I have given her the name that is carved on her gravestone but her birth-name was Skarbek and her surname Gizycki, in the Dictionary of National Biography, is that of her second husband (whom she divorced after the Second World War). Krystyna is often called Christine Granville, which is the English name that she adopted. Her date of birth is given on her gravestone as May 1 1915, but Ron Nowicki has come across a travel visa in Poland, in which Krystyna's father described her year of birth as 1908, and he has also seen three documents signed by Krystyna in which her birth year is given as 1909. It might be that she just chose the year 1915 when she adopted the identity and papers of 'Christine Granville' in the course of her escape from Budapest, planned in the British Consulate there, as described below.

Krystyna was born in her maternal grandparents' house in Warsaw, the second child, after her brother Andrzej, to Count Jerzy Skarbek and his wife Stefania (née Goldfeder) who was from a rich, banking family of assimilated Jewish descent.

In 1920, after the First World War, the family moved to her mother's estate of Trzepnica, near Piotrków, where Krystyna, something of a 'wild child', learned to ride astride and to race with reckless abandon as well as to ski. One of her biographers, Madeleine Masson, suggests that Krystyna was (in her own words), from an early age, marked by a 'recalcitrant' nature; all, in the usual way, probably because of an education in Roman Catholic boarding schools. The family moved back to Warsaw in 1928, and Krystyna persuaded her mother to let her take a job with a motor dealer (Polska Fiat) but this was not a great success. Aged eighteen she left the job and briefly married Karol Getlich, of German descent, but they were incompatible and the marriage was swiftly dissolved by mutual consent. Krystyna's father, to whom she had been very close, died in 1930.

Krystyna then met a Polish diplomat, called Jerzy Gizycki, on a skiing holiday near her beloved Zakopane. He was captivated by her fine-boned gracefulness and her dark-haired beauty, and she married him on November 2 1938, after which he was appointed Polish Consul in Addis Ababa. He and Krystyna were stationed when Hitler invaded Poland on September 1 1939. This made them decide to move to London and to attempt to save their families but, by this time, the marriage was on the rocks and they soon became voluntarily estranged and separated. Gizycki discovered Krystyna's affair with Andrew Kennedy in 1941, and he left England for Canada. Krystyna divorced him in 1946 and he died in Mexico in 1973.

Owing to her adventurous spirit and her friendship with *Guardian* journalist Frederick Voigt, it was not long before Krystyna, in England, was introduced by him to Sir Robert Vansittart and George Taylor of section D of the recently formed Secret Intelligence Service ('SIS'). Taylor, on Vansittart's recommendation, formally signed her up to work for Section D.

In February 1940, she started making skiing incursions from Budapest, over the Tatra mountains, and on across Slovakia into Poland. Krystyna even persuaded Olympic skier Jan Marusarz to accompany her. She carried propaganda literature and gathered information. Her mother insisted on staying in the country and was later murdered by the Nazis; ironically in the very prison (Pawiak), which Krystyna's prison-reforming great-great uncle (Fryderyk Florian Skarbek, incidentally Chopin's godfather), had designed. After incarceration during the War, her brother died in 1950. Upon learning of his release from a prison camp in 1945, Krystyna had tried to help him by sending food and things that he might need.

Section D had been, overall, a damp squib. William McKenzies's history of the SOE shows that there had been plans for an unnamed intelligence bureau, independent of MI5 and MI6, as far back as 1938. The idea was formed between people such as Lords Halifax and Hankey and Colonel 'Jo' Holland. Section D had been the first result.

Once Churchill became Prime Minister, they approached him with the idea of what became the SOE and he approved it and that is why it is sometimes called 'Churchill's Secret Army', even though he did not originate the idea for it. Neville Chamberlain drafted the charter and came up with the name for the SOE. It was officially formed on July 22 1940 'To set Europe ablaze', and its students and graduates ('Bods') were, sometimes, known as the 'Hush Hush Troops'. The SOE had headquarters at 64 Baker Street, a 'finishing school' for agents on the Beaulieu estate, and training centres around the country. Owing especially to her service to date, and her fluency in French, Krystyna was one of the first agents recruited and accepted into the AMF section.

In the spring of 1941 Krystyna hurriedly left Budapest as she was being pursued by the Hungarian Secret Police and the Gestapo, and it was then that she changed her name and birth date in her new British papers.

The most impressive feat, attributed to her, by this stage, was playing a part in transmitting the intelligence that Hitler was concentrating forces on the Russian border. This enabled Churchill to warn Stalin of the impending invasion of Russia ('Operation Barbarossa', which happened on June 22 1941). For this, Krystyna attracted the description 'Churchill's favourite spy', but whether he was actually very aware of her specific identity in this respect is uncertain, because, in fact, the intelligence was gathered by others and merely passed to her as an external courier, by the Polish Musketeer resistance network and then passed up the management line by her. By this time Krystyna was on her way to Palestine and she gave the information to Aidan Crawley in Sofia, who sent it on to Churchill.

It is very uncertain (although much vaunted, even to the extent of an alleged affair), whether there was any, let alone any close, link at all between Krystyna and Ian Fleming. But being in the Naval Intelligence Service himself, he could easily have been well enough aware of Krystyna to lend colour to the suggestion that he had roughly based the characters Vesper Lynd (in the first James Bond novel *Casino Royale*, in 1953) and Tatiana Romanova (in *From Russia With Love*) on her.

Krystyna made the trip into Poland twice out of four attempts, liaising (as mentioned above), with the Polish underground network the Musketeers. On one of these occasions, she was arrested by Slovak border guards but (according to her own account), showing a glint of the cool courage that she would wield so effectively later on, she talked her companion and herself out of it.

Whether or not she had ever sworn an oath of allegiance to the British Crown, the Polish Government in Exile mistrusted her. A Polish intelligence agent put about a rumour that she was a double agent and they tried to persuade the British to stop using her on active service. There were times when even the British also suspected her because of the apparent ease with which she accomplished her missions and travelled behind enemy lines.

On duty in Budapest she met a childhood friend called Andrzeij Kowerski. He was also on the run from enemy authorities and escaped with her, bearing papers arranged for him by the British Consulate in the name of 'Andrew Kennedy'.

Krystyna and Kennedy became an 'item' and travelled together to Constantinople and Cairo, living in hotels. In January 1941, they were arrested in Budapest by the Gestapo but Krystyna used the ploy of biting her tongue until it bled, coughed out blood and claimed to have tuberculosis, convincingly enough to win their release. They then made their way to Cairo via the Balkans, Turkey, Syria and the Lebanon.

Krystyna's most famous *coup de main* occurred towards the end of the War. Over the night of 6–7 July 1944, she was parachuted into France to become a courier to the half-Belgian, half-English Francis Cammaerts (code name 'Roger') whose 'Jockey' network (by which Krystyna was code-named 'Pauline Armand' and 'Madame Pauline'), was responsible for resistance and sabotage east of the Rhône. In fact, Cammaerts had started out in the War as a registered conscientious objector and had consequently lost his job as a schoolmaster and been put to farm labour. When his brother was killed on active duty in the RAF, he changed his mind and joined Section F of the SOE. Cammaerts was trained before being parachuted into Compiègne, France, over the night of 23–24 March 1943 but, on landing, he realised that resistance in the area was too hazardous to be effective and moved south to the Riviera where he founded the 'Jockey' resistance network and became a most effective saboteur after the June 1944 allied landings. Part of the secret of his success seems to have been his elusiveness, which he reinforced by always contacting members of his network, rather than letting them contact him.

Krystyna's function was to help Cammaerts link up the French Maquis (the underground French resistance movement) and the Italian partisans in anticipation of the allied landings in the South of France, and to turn Polish conscripts to the Nazi army back to the allied cause. On August 13 1944, just before the allied landings, Cammaerts, Xan Fielding and a French officer called Sorensen, were arrested by the Gestapo at a snap roadblock, condemned to death as spies and imprisoned in the spa town of Digne-les-Bains, pending their execution. Krystyna learned of their plight and, unarmed, went to see Captain Albert Schenck, a French liaison gendarme (and Nazi collaborator), between the Vichy French and the Gestapo. She introduced herself (effectively disclosing that she was a British spy), as the niece of Field Marshal Bernard Montgomery and as Cammaerts's wife. She said that the allies were advancing and pointed out that if the prisoners were harmed the reprisals would be swift and terrible. She added the incentive of a bribe of two million francs, although who raised the subject is not very clear. Schenck arranged for her to meet a Gestapo officer called Max Waem at Schenck's house and Krystyna repeated her points. Waem's reaction was to agree to the release of the men and decide to leave the prison himself.

The bribe for Schenck was delivered by air from Algiers but Schenck (ignoring Cammaerts's advice to leave the area), was later killed in the town. The prisoners were released and Krystyna met the astonished men with refreshments that included brandy and cigarettes and (together with her voluntary Gestapo prisoner, Max Waem) they drove to safety behind allied lines.

Krystyna was not deployed again and ended the war as an Honorary Flying Officer. She later said that at the time she went to Schenck and Waem, she had been unaware of the risk that she had been taking and that it was only afterwards that she had appreciated it. She was awarded the George Medal in January 1945 for her actions at Digne-les-Bains, as well as the Croix de Guerre, by France and, in May 1947, she was also made an Officer of The British Empire, a rank above the usual rank of Member of The British Empire, for her service rank.

Krystyna's SOE records in the National Archives run under file reference HS 9/612 (including her War Office service), down to December 31 1946, and include the recommendation, dated 10 December 1944, of Major-General W.A.M. Stawell CBE, MC, in relation to Krystyna under the name Mary Christine Granville. I paraphrase, except where speech marks appear. The following account of what happened, in relation to her last mission, appears to have come from Krystyna at the time.

Stawell referred to her as a Polish patriot of high integrity who had been employed for four years on work of the most dangerous nature inside occupied Europe. Her work had been remarkable and of the greatest value to the Allied cause. On the night of 6–7 July 1944 she was infiltrated into Southern France by parachute to act as liaison officer to the chief British field officer in the area. Her task was to work on the possibility of subverting satellite enemy troops (conscripts from conquered countries).

Krystyna started work immediately and reported that the possibilities were considerable. On 17th July the area commander asked for her to be given an assistant owing to the progress that she had made.

He goes on to describe how, when the D-Day landings took place in June 1944 and the battle for the Vercors Plateau was fought between the Maquis and the Nazis, Krystyna remained for the battle and then escaped with the Free French General. Afterwards, she continued with her work of subverting satellite troops. The Polish troops at Briançon were prepared to surrender to the Maquis, subject to conditions. From Vercors, Krystyna went to Col de Larche on the Italian frontier and effected an important liaison with Colonel Marzzalani of the Italian Maquis, and then moved to Northern Italy where she was frequently under fire for two weeks. He describes the capture of Cammaerts and his colleagues and how it was a serious blow, especially as it occurred two days before the planned Allied invasion of the South of France. Stawell noted that Krystyna immediately took over the whole work of the mission until a new commanding officer arrived when she had fully briefed him. She had single-handedly set about securing the release of the three men. She spent three days finding out the size of the guard with a view to organising a raid on the prison:

'...........*but when this was found to be impracticable she, alone, and fully appreciating the risk that she ran [in fact Krystyna later said that, at the time, she had not appreciated the risk at all] and that, on paper her task would appear impossible, went to the prison to see the head of the Gestapo himself, and in the Gestapo office was interviewed by all the Gestapo officers, except one, a total of eight, each of whom entered the room armed and by that time, were aware that she was an enemy agent, and fully intending to arrest her. In spite of all these things however, by a series of amazing stories and threats, she persuaded one of their number to release all three of the officers, even though each of them had already been condemned to death as enemy agents and were due to be shot 12 hours afterwards.*

The nerve, coolness, and devotion to duty and high courage of this lady which inspired and brought to successful conclusion this astonishing coup de main must certainly be considered as one of the most remarkable personal exploits of the war and in the particular circumstances I have the honour to recommend that her courage be recognised by the immediate award of the George Cross.

This recommendation was then sent to Field Marshal H. R. Alexander, Supreme Allied Commander, who endorsed it with 'I recommend the award of the OBE'. As a result, she received both the George Medal and the OBE and the recommendation is also endorsed with 'OBE (because GM)'. Plainly, the endorsement by Alexander indicated his approval of the higher George Cross with an additional OBE (Military Division). It is unclear to me why she was denied the George Cross, for how many would dare, not suddenly, in the heat of battle, but after consideration of the options, to do as she had done: coolly walking, unarmed into the face of the enemy and then, by force of personality alone, forcing such a truly marvellous result?

After being demobbed with one month's pay, Krystyna found herself homeless, penniless, jobless and, but for the tardy granting of British citizenship, on November 23 1946, stateless, and she drifted through dead-end jobs including as a telephonist at India House and as an assistant in the dress department at Harrods. Eventually, maybe seeking all the adventure that peacetime could give her, she joined the Shaw Savill shipping line as a stewardess (between November 23 1946 and May 1951), where she met a fellow employee called Dennis George Muldowney, a lonely, unstable, forty-one year old divorcé , on the liner *Rauhine* and became friends with him. But friendship was not enough for Muldowney and he relentlessly pursued her.

Even if the modern laws against harassment had then existed, it is unlikely that Krystyna would have been the type to have invoked them and she simply evaded Muldowney; ultimately moving to the *Winchester Castle* in the Union Castle shipping line to escape his company.

Krystyna even made arrangements to leave London on 16th June 1952, to go to Kennedy (with whom she had reconciled, following a breach) in Germany, presumably hoping for a fresh start and a brighter post-war future. Maybe Muldowney, who had taken a job as a porter at the Reform Club, suspected that she was leaving because on the evening of 15th June he tracked her down to the Shellbourne Hotel at 1–3 Lexham Gardens, Earls Court, and, according to his written confession on arrest, had waited outside for her.

He saw Krystyna go inside, confronted her in the foyer and asked for the return of letters he had sent her, but she replied that she had burned them. He disbelieved her. Krystyna then told him that she wanted nothing to do with him; that she was off to the continent, and that he would see her in two years' time.

According to another report, she called out, 'Get him off me!' and a hotel employee rushed to help her, but in an act both premeditated and frenzied, Muldowney drew a sheath knife from his hip pocket and stabbed her – up to the hilt – in the heart.

After all that she had been through and all that she had accomplished and with such a fearless, dashing spirit, Krystyna's end was to fall and die as a result of such a desperate act, in the foyer of a small hotel.

She was, though, buried with honour in her many decorations. A spadeful of Polish earth was laid on her coffin (now beneath an imposing monument), in St Mary's Roman Catholic Cemetery at Kensal Green.

Muldowney was arraigned on September 11 1952 at the Central Criminal Court and, declining all legal assistance, pleaded guilty to Krystyna's murder. He said, 'To kill is the final possession'. Muldowney was hanged in Pentonville Prison on 30th September 1952. No one seems to have considered that he was insane by virtue of an overwhelming, passionate obsession.

When he died in 1988, Andrew Kennedy's ashes were brought back from Munich and interred at the foot of Krystyna's grave.

There are various claims surrounding Krystyna's life after the war, such as the one already mentioned; that she was introduced to Ian Fleming. One claim condescends to the specificity that they met in Bertorelli's restaurant in Charlotte Street, Covent Garden, where they discussed possible work for her. I have tried to establish whether this (or any other meeting) did take place but I have had no positive result, and this is supported by the researches of Fleming biographer Andrew Lycett, and Krystyna researcher Ron Nowicki. Moreover, surely, if she had been in a position to ask Ian Fleming to help her to find suitable work, then (with all her language skills and his many contacts throughout the Establishment, including the Kelmsley newspaper group, for which he was Foreign Manager on *The Sunday Times*), it is extremely unlikely indeed that she would have ended her days as a stewardess on an ocean liner.

Xan Fielding, one of those whom she had saved at Digne-les-Bains, dedicated his book *Hide and Seek* 'To the memory of Christine Granville' and made it very clear that as far as he was concerned, Krystyna had been let down after the war by the nation she had served so bravely and so well. Maybe the gritty truth is that peacetime had no obvious use for her recklessly heroic qualities and she was just disregarded as another refugee in need of work.

However, if you ever venture into the bar of Dukes Hotel in St James's, this woman of spirit, beauty and dash has another memorial, because bar manager, Alessandro Palazzi, in tribute to Krystyna, now uses Potocki Polish vodka in his excellent version of the Vesper Martini. We don't know whether or not Krystyna really was the template for Vesper Lynd or Tatiana Romanova, but we do know Dukes Hotel bar was, after all, the place where Ian Fleming picked up, from the 1950s' bar manager, the James Bond catch phrase, 'shaken not stirred'.

The Dukes Vesper Martini though, rather after Krystyna's own spirit is, actually, neither shaken nor stirred.

Chapter 22

Major-General Sir Fitzroy Hew Royle Maclean, of Strachur and Glensluian Bart, (1911–1996) KT, CBE, 15th Hereditary Keeper and Captain of Dunconnel Castle

White on a throne or guarded in a cave
There lives a prophet who can understand
Why men were born: but surely we are brave,
Who take the Golden Road to Samarkand.

From *The Golden Journey to Samarkand*
by John Elroy Flecker

SIR FITZROY Hew Royle Maclean was a near contemporary of Ian Fleming and their time at Eton overlapped. His reputation as a soldier on secret wartime missions, especially in his assistance to Marshal Tito and his Yugoslav partisans, was said by some to have been part of the inspiration for James Bond. His later perceptiveness in understanding Mikhail Gorbachev enabled him to advise the Iron Lady to work on Gorbachev, so bringing about the eventual lifting of the Iron Curtain; much of it all then flowing from Margaret Thatcher's memorable pronouncement, 'I like Mr Gorbachev. We can do business.'

The Macleans' ancestral home was Duart Castle on the Isle of Mull, but Fitzroy Maclean was born in Cairo on 11 March 1911, to Major Charles Wilberforce Maclean and Frances Elaine (née Royle). The Macleans were an old, martial, Scottish family and had fought the Jacobite cause. Maclean spent his early years between Scotland and Italy and became fluent in several languages. After Eton, he spent a year in Germany and then went up to King's College, Cambridge, emerging with a second class honours degree in history in 1932.

Maclean entered the diplomatic service in 1933 and started in the Foreign Office in London before he was moved to be third Secretary in the British Embassy in Paris in October 1934. In 1937 he preferred to be sent to Moscow, rather than Washington, and was appointed Second Secretary. He used some of his time to travel and look around, simply for personal information, and was followed by Stalin's secret police, the NKVD. Maclean penetrated places such as Samarkand, Bokhara, Tashkent, Batum and Tiflis. He witnessed the murderous purges and 'trials' by Stalin of the old Bolsheviks. He even realised that there would be the Nazi-Soviet pact that was announced on 31 August 1939, clearing the way for Hitler to invade Poland, without Russian opposition. He was brought back to London and then he sat at the Russian desk, tapping his feet, impatient for active service, but his was a reserved occupation and he could not leave. However, he realised in 1941 that, if he were elected a member of parliament, he would have to resign his office. He managed to be adopted as the Conservative candidate for Lancaster and did resign, enlisting in the Queen's Own Cameron Highlanders as a private soldier. He was soon commissioned as a second Lieutenant and won a by-election to become MP for Lancaster in October 1941.

Maclean was sent on a mission to Cairo to meet David Stirling who had founded the Special Air Service ('SAS'), to go behind enemy lines and carry out sabotage. He joined the First SAS regiment in January 1942 as a Lieutenant. In fact, it turned out to be involved less with an air service than with jeeps in which the saboteurs (including Maclean's colleague Ralph A. Bagnold), would infiltrate, through the desert (after the fashion of T. E. Lawrence), and go behind enemy lines with their bombs and weapons to create as much mayhem as they could, before withdrawing. According to his obituary in the *Daily Telegraph*on 18 June 1996, Maclean once went on a mission to Benghazi with Randolph Churchill but they were stopped by an Italian sentry. Thinking fast, Maclean demanded to see the guard commander and gave him a telling off in fluent Italian for not having stopped them before, as they might have been British agents on an armed sabotage mission. The guard commander said that this was fanciful!

Maclean was then injured in a car accident, as a result of Stirling's appalling driving ('David Stirling's driving was the most dangerous thing in World War II') but when he recovered he had another go at Benghazi and then even kidnapped the German Consul in Axis-controlled Iraq (leading to German withdrawal) and, after the desert campaign, he arrested the pro-Nazi Governor-General of Esfahan, General Zahidi. These exploits, along with the kidnapping by Patrick Leigh Fermor and his SOE team, in April 1944, of the German commander of Crete, considerably helped British morale as well as strategy.

Maclean made Captain in 1942 and Lieutenant-Colonel in 1943.

In July 1943, as a result of the exploits described above, Churchill decided that Maclean had all the right qualities and experience to be sent, as his personal envoy, on a mission to Marshal Tito and his partisans in Yugoslavia, who were engaged in enthusiastically fighting the Nazis, unlike the Chetniks who were suspected of collaboration. As Maclean put it, the mission was 'simply to find out who was killing the most Germans and suggest the manner by which we could help them to kill more.'

Maclean was soon won over by Tito's abilities and he stayed for two years on a fast-track promotion to Brigadier ('The Balkan Brigadier'), in difficult circumstances, combatting various rivalries, difficulties with supplies, as well as the fear of ultimate Russian ambitions on the Adriatic coast. Oddly enough, Maclean was hindered, rather than helped, by the presence in his team of the equally obstreperous Randolph Churchill and the novelist Evelyn Waugh (who disliked communism so much that he evolved a peculiar theory that Tito was, in fact, a young woman).

Maclean's help and influence probably buoyed Tito up enough to enable him not only to secure triumph in the Battle of Belgrade in October 1944, but also to successfully resist Soviet influence after the War; even though Yugoslavia became a communist state, at least it was independent. It must be said, however, that the long-term political outcome for Yugoslavia was not upper-most in British minds at the time that Tito was helped. The British simply wished to help the Yugoslav group which would be most effective against Nazi control of the Balkans.

Fitzroy Maclean received the Croix de Guerre from France, the CBE (Military division), the Yugoslav Partisan star (1st Class), the Russian Order of Kutuzov, and later on, the Order of Merit (Yugoslavia) in 1969, and the Order of the Yugoslav Star and Ribbon in 1981. In 1993 he was made a Knight of the Most Ancient and Most Noble Order of the Thistle. He was one of the very few foreigners permitted to own property in Yugoslavia during its communist era and kept an island villa there.

After the War, as a Major-General, Maclean was put in charge of refugee commissions and displaced persons' camps at various locations through Europe. After he had completed that tour of duty, he took up his seat in parliament (where he never made much of a mark as a parliamentarian), and married Veronica, daughter of Lord Lovat, and widow of a naval officer, who brought him a stepson and a stepdaughter, as well as giving him two sons of their own. He was made a baronet in July 1957, although he remained MP for Lancaster until 1959 and then for Bute and Ayrshire until February 1974.

In 1949 Maclean wrote his best-selling memoirs *Eastern Approaches*, as well as later books on Russia and his beloved Scotland.

In the 1980s he even ventured into tele-journalism and made films about Russia which enabled him to inform himself about the then state of that place and thus, he was able to inform and advise the British government, as already mentioned, of the possibilities presented, in the mid-1980s, by the leadership of Mikhail Gorbachev.

Tall, brave, genial and gallant, Maclean enjoyed the material tastes of James Bond, although he has been likened more to John Buchan's Richard Hannay. However, he enjoyed the Bond association and used to joke about it with his wife, especially when making Martinis. He also had a collection of early editions of the Bond novels.

Maclean died during a visit to Hitchin, Hertfordshire on 15 June 1996.

Chapter 23

Noor-un-Nisa Inayat Khan GC, MBE, Croix de Guerre (1914–1944)

I wish some Indians would win high military distinction in this war. If one or two could do something in the Allied service, which was very brave and which everybody admired it would help to make a bridge between the English people and the Indians.

Noor-un-Nisa Inayat Khan

SHE did just that. Noor was the eldest of four children born to Hazrat Inayat Khan and his wife Ora Ray Baker, in Russia, on 2 January 1914. Her father was a Sufi lecturer and musician, descended from Tipu Sultan, the last Mughal Emperor of Mysore, and her mother was an Anglo-American, whom her father had met on a trip to the United States.

Noor's father died in 1927, and she had to take added responsibility for her mother and her younger siblings. Noor, at this time, was described as quiet, shy, sensitive, and gentle, and she lived with the family at Suresnes, in the western suburbs of Paris, during the 1920s and 1930s, and studied child psychology at the Sorbonne. She also had musical studies at the Conservatoire de Paris.

In 1939, Noor published *Twenty Jakata Tales*, which were accounts of certain Buddhist legends, for children.

Although Noor had been influenced by the pacifist teachings of her Sufi father, after the family fled France to escape the Nazis, she decided to do whatever she could to defeat Nazism. So, on 19 November 1940, she joined the Women's Auxiliary Air Force (WAAF) and, as an Aircraftwoman 2nd Class, she was sent to be trained as a wireless operator.

After being assigned to a bomber training school in June 1941, she applied for a commission.

In the autumn of 1942, she was approached and then recruited to join Section (F) (France) of the SOE and, in early February 1943, she was posted to the Air Ministry, Directorate of Air Intelligence, seconded to First Aid Nursing Yeomanry (FANY), and sent, first, to Wanborough Manor, near Guildford in Surrey, and from there to various other SOE schools for training; including those at Winterfold, Boarmans and Thame Park. During her training (which was never completed), she adopted the name Nora Baker.

Some of those in charge of her held mixed opinions about her psychological suitability for secret warfare. Nevertheless, she had the important support of Vera Atkins of the SOE and her fluency in the French language and her training in wireless operation made her a desirable candidate for service behind enemy lines, in Nazi-occupied France.

On the night of 16–17 June 1943, codenamed 'Madeleine' and under the cover of the French identity of Jeanne-Marie Regnier, Assistant Section Officer and Ensign, Noor was flown to a landing ground, in Northern France on a night-landing double Lysander aircraft operation. She was met by Henri Dericourt, a former French pilot and member of the SOE.

Noor travelled to Paris, and together with two other women (Diana Rowden, codenamed 'Paulette', and Cecily Lefort, codenamed 'Alice'), Noor joined the Physician network led by Francis Suttill, codenamed 'Prosper'.

She did not know it yet but the security of the network had already been seriously compromised and, very shortly after her arrival, all other Physician network radio operators were arrested by the Nazi *Sicherheitsdienst* (security agency) ('SD'). In spite of the evident danger, Noor rejected an offer to return to England, at least until a replacement could be sent, and she continued transmitting as the last remaining link between London and Paris.

Moving from place to place, she managed to escape capture while maintaining wireless communication with London. She refused to abandon what had become the most important and dangerous under-cover post in France and she did excellent work.

Finally, Noor was probably betrayed to the Germans; possibly by either Henri Dericourt or by Renée Garry. Dericourt (codenamed Gilbert) was an SOE officer and former French Air Force pilot who has been suspected of working as a double agent for the German Abler (Defence). Renée Garry was the sister of Emile Garry, Noor's organiser in the Physician network, and might have had reason to be jealous of her.

On about 13 October 1943 Noor was arrested at her flat and then interrogated at the notorious SD Headquarters at 84 Avenue Foch, in

Paris. During her arrest she fought so ferociously that even the brutal SD officers were frightened of her and she was treated as a dangerous prisoner. There is no evidence of her being tortured, but her interrogation lasted over a month. During that time, she twice attempted to escape. Hans Kieffer, the former head of Gestapo in Paris, testified after the war that she did not give the Gestapo a single piece of information, but lied consistently.

The SD found her papers, amongst which she had kept, contrary to instructions (and rather stupidly), copies of the messages she had sent as an SOE radio operative. Although she refused to reveal any secret codes, the Germans gained enough information from the cache to continue to send and receive messages, using her identity and apparatus.

The British failed to properly investigate evident anomalies in the transmissions (which should have indicated they were sent under enemy control) and, consequently, three more agents sent to France were captured by the Germans at their parachute landings, among them Madeleine Damerment, who was later murdered with Noor.

On 25 November 1943 Noor escaped from the SD Headquarters along with fellow SOE Agents John Renshaw Starr and Leon Faye but, owing to an air raid and a roll call, they were soon missed and then re-captured in the immediate vicinity.

After refusing to sign a declaration not to make further escape attempts, Noor was taken to Pforzheim prison in Germany on 27 November 1943 'for safe keeping' and imprisoned in solitary confinement as a so-called Nacht und Nebel ('night and fog') prisoner – a prisoner (especially a resistance fighter or agent), arrested and kept without any contact with the outside world and in complete secrecy, pending their murder and disappearance without trace, according to a directive from Hitler in 1941.

As she was classified as 'highly dangerous', she was even handcuffed and shackled in chains most of the time. As the prison director testified after the war, Noor remained uncooperative and continued to refuse to give any information on her work or her fellow agents.

On 10 September 1944 Noor Inayat Khan and three other SOE agents (Yolande Beekman, Eliane Plewman and Madeleine Damerment), were taken to Karlsruhe prison. The next day, they were moved to the Dachau Concentration Camp.

During the night of 12–13 September 1944, the four women were taken outside and shot in the back of the head. A former Dachau prisoner later came forward and said that Noor was first cruelly beaten by a sadistic SS soldier called Friedrich Wilhelm Ruppert and that her last words had been to shout: 'La Liberté!' As modern societies whittle away at Liberty, on any old excuse, ranging from our own health and the need to protect us from ourselves, to the need to protect us all from the vague threat of terrorism, by the 'authorities' treating everyone as a suspect, we might occasionally pause to consider how many people have actually given their lives to protect Liberty – something far more precious than the 'safety' to be found in all the smokeless zones and all the airport body searches in the world.

The women were cremated in the notorious death camp and their remains were never recovered. Ruppert was later convicted of war crimes and hanged in 1946.

Noor Inayat Khan was posthumously awarded a Mention in Dispatches and a French Croix de Guerre. She was the third of three World War II FANY members to be awarded the George Cross, Britain's second highest award for gallantry (the other two were Violette Szabo, also dealt with later, and Odette Sansom Hallowes (Churchill), who survived the War).

I have never really understood why Noor and Violette were not awarded the Victoria Cross. It is often said that the Victoria Cross is awarded only for action in battle but this is not actually so: it is confined to 'action in the face of the enemy'. So far as I can see, unarmed and shackled women who persist in refusing to assist the enemy under various degrees of 'interrogation', even torture and who are facing certain death, are at least as courageous as those others who have won the Victoria Cross in armed battle. Equally, I do not understand why Krystyna Skarbek-Granville was denied the George Cross (for which she was recommended). After all, she had walked, voluntarily and unarmed, into the face of the enemy (and the Gestapo at that), disclosed her status as an enemy agent, and instead of being shot as a spy, she even prevailed in obtaining the freedom of Gestapo prisoners.

Maybe, there is some small hope that there might, one day, be a review of their decorations and appropriate advancements made.

The citation for Noor's GC appeared in the *London Gazette* on 5 April 1949, and reads as follows:

'The KING has been graciously pleased to approve the posthumous award of the GEORGE CROSS to:—

Assistant Section Officer Nora INAYAT-KHAN (9901), Women's Auxiliary Air Force.

Assistant Section Officer Nora INAYAT-KHAN was the first woman operator to be infiltrated into enemy occupied France, and was landed by Lysander aircraft on 16th June, 1943. During the weeks immediately following her arrival, the Gestapo made mass arrests in

the Paris Resistance groups to which she had been detailed. She refused however to abandon what had become the principal and most dangerous post in France, although given the opportunity to return to England, because she did not wish to leave her French comrades without communications and she hoped also to rebuild her group. She remained at her post therefore and did the excellent work which earned her a posthumous Mention in Despatches.

The Gestapo had a full description of her, but knew only her code name "Madeleine". They deployed considerable forces in their effort to catch her and so break the last remaining link with London. After 3 months she was betrayed to the Gestapo and taken to their H.Q. in the Avenue Foch. The Gestapo had found her codes and messages and were now in a position to work back to London. They asked her to co-operate, but she refused and gave them no information of any kind. She was imprisoned in one of the cells on the 5th floor of the Gestapo H.Q. and remained there for several weeks during which time she made two unsuccessful attempts at escape. She was asked to sign a declaration that she would make no further attempts but she refused and the Chief of the Gestapo obtained permission from Berlin to send her to Germany for "safe custody". She was the first agent to be sent to Germany.

Assistant Section Officer INAYAT-KHAN was sent to Karlsruhe in November; 1943, and then to Pforzheim, where her cell was apart from the main prison. She was considered to be a particularly dangerous and unco-operative prisoner. The Director of the prison has also been interrogated and has confirmed that Assistant Section Officer INAYAT-KHAN, when interrogated by the Karlsruhe Gestapo, refused to give any information whatsoever, either as to her work or her colleagues.

She was taken with three others to Dachau Camp on the 12th September, 1944. On arrival, she was taken to the crematorium and shot.

Assistant Section Officer INAYAT-KHAN displayed the most conspicuous courage, both moral and physical over a period of more than 12 months.'

Sometimes, much is made of the fact that the life of a shy, young, Indian girl of a princely family was sacrificed in the cause of Liberty but, at the end of the day, her line of descent neither adds to, nor detracts from, her acts of valour.

There is a current proposal to erect an individual monument (apart from the official group monuments), to her in London. There is also a plaque to her memory at Dachau.

Chapter 24

Tenzing Norgay GM (1914–1986)

'It has been a long road from a mountain coolie, a bearer of loads, to a wearer of a coat with rows of medals, who is carried about in 'planes and worries about income tax.'

Tenzing Norgay

T HE SHERPAS ('eastern people') are a distinct ethnic group, living high in the Himalayan mountains of Nepal, and they speak their own language and mainly follow Buddhism. They might once have been nomadic people, who moved around according to the seasonal finding of pasture and there are four main clans. There is controversy whether they ever migrated to their present homeland but, by the nineteenth century, they had autonomy within the fairly new state of Nepal.

They are recognised as strong, expert, cheerful climbers, with especial physical and psychological aptitude and endurance for climbing at high altitude. Since at least the 1920s they have been recognised as most important to the survival of expeditions up Mount Everest; which Sherpas call 'Choalungma' or 'Goddess Mother of The Land'. They still consider the mountain as the abode of the gods; although they no longer regard its upper parts as off-limits to humans. The Sherpas placate the gods before climbing there with a Puja ceremony, in which they pay homage and make offerings.

At first, Sherpas were used as porters, as they could manage to carry loads of eighty pounds at twenty-five thousand feet, but they were soon climbing too, later competing for the Tiger Medal and a consequential pay increase for high altitude porterage. George Mallory reported to the joint meeting of the RGS and the Alpine Club that the 1922 expedition owed most to the Sherpas' endurance to carry loads to sustain the high-camp method of the expedition. Moreover, seven Sherpas perished in that attempt. However, despite fatalities, the Sherpas have kept at it, not least because their climbing feats raise world awareness of the people in this remote region, as well as much-needed revenue.

In 1963 there was the first US expedition and the climbers were debilitated by frostbite on their descent. Teams of four Sherpas rescued each of them and carried them for two days to Namche Bazaar, where they could be airlifted away. Indeed, the Sherpa teams, despite the circumstances, even raced each other down! Of the first one hundred fatalities that the mountain has claimed, forty-one have been Sherpas.

Tenzing Norgay (Sherpa Tenzing) was born in May 1914, in the Kharta Valley in Tibet where his mother was staying, as the eleventh of thirteen children. The family's home was, in fact, in the Thami Solu Khumbu region of Nepal. He was sent to the monastery to train to be a monk but ran away and, after that, he had no schooling but just farmed with his family. He remained illiterate but did learn to speak several languages, including Nepalese, Tibetan, English and Hindi.

Early in life Norgay heard of the stories of expeditions on the mountain and developed his own passion to climb it and find out about it for himself. He went to Katmandu but found no work and, at the age of eighteen, went to Darjeeling, hoping to be selected as a porter on an Everest expedition. He was not immediately successful and took a number of labouring jobs, marrying Dawa Phut, by whom he had two surviving daughters. Then he was chosen by Eric Shipton for an expedition in 1935. He also made expeditions in 1936 and 1938, winning a Tiger medal in 1938. These expeditions were up the northern, Tibetan side.

From 1939, through the Second World War, he served as an army cook and batman on the North West Frontier of India. Dawa died in 1944 and he returned to Darjeeling and eventually married Ang Lahmu. In 1947 Norgay went on a Canadian expedition (which turned back owing to a storm).

He also spent time as a personal assistant, journeyed to western Nepal, and undertook several mountain expeditions, including an attempt on Nanga Parbat and the actual ascent of Nanda Deri in 1951. By this time, Norgay was a head porter. In 1952, a Swiss expedition made him head porter and full climbing member of the team. On this occasion, he took his team of porters up the Lhotse Face to Everest's south col and, on 28 May 1952, he and Raymond Lambert reached a then record 28,200 feet.

In 1953, Norgay was a member of Colonel John Hunt's expedition, Norgay's own seventh outing on the mountain, and he saved Edmund Hillary in a fall. The expedition then set out in March 1953 for the South col and made a final camp at 25,900 feet. On 26 May an attempt at the summit by others failed and Hunt then chose Hillary and Norgay to have a go. They set out on 28 May and pitched a final tent at 27,900 feet. They advanced to the 40ft face (now called Hillary's Step) where Hillary managed to wedge himself, and proceeded to the top, at 29,028 feet. They stayed there for only fifteen minutes and Hillary took the famous photograph of Norgay. Norgay later said that Hillary had refused to let him take Hillary's picture but Hillary said that Norgay did not know how to use a camera and that was not the place to teach him.

There was a certain amount of tension between the men over the ascent and Norgay complained that Hillary blamed him for the difficulties that they encountered, but took credit for the rest. However, they did remain friends.

In any event, in June 1953, he and Edmund Hillary gave Queen Elizabeth II the best coronation gift that she could have wished for: the official announcement that, together, they had conquered Everest on 29 May 1953. Norgay had made an offering to the gods and had his photograph taken flying various national flags and the flag of the UN from his ice pick.

There has since been controversy surrounding which of them was first to the top. Their joint position was that they had made it together, although Norgay later claimed that Hillary had been first up. Norgay received the Order of the Star of Nepal (tara) 1st Class, and many other awards from several countries for his achievement. The Queen gave Hillary a knighthood but Prime Minister of India, Nehru, forbade the acceptance of a knighthood by Norgay (disdaining it as 'the confetti of Empire') and he was given the George Medal for gallantry instead.

In 1954 Nehru did though, appoint him to be director of field training of the Himalayan Mountain Institute in Darjeeling, which is where Norgay made his home. He married a third time and had three sons and a daughter. He also engaged in certain commercial ventures but when he was forcibly retired from the Institute in 1976, he carried on as a guide. He wrote two books (mentioned in the bibliography) and died of complications from bronchitis on 9 May 1986. His ashes are buried at the Institute from which he felt that he had been retired in breach of Nehru's original promise that he would hold his directorship for life.

If Sir Francis Younghusband had lived to see the day of the conquest of Everest he would have needed to have found some other unfulfilled, aspirational challenge!

Since 1953, Everest has been climbed many times, even twice in the same week, and some of Norgay's own descendants have also been 'on top of the world'.

Chapter 25

Violette Reine Elizabeth Szabo GC, MBE, Croix de Guerre (1921–1945)

The life that I have
Is all that I have
And the life that I have
Is yours.

The love that I have
Of the life that I have
Is yours and yours and yours.

A sleep I shall have
A rest I shall have
Yet death will be but a pause.

For the peace of my years
In the long green grass
Will be yours and yours and yours.

The Life That I Have, a poem by Leo Marks

THE ABOVE poem was given by the poet (himself an SOE agent) to the twenty-three-year-old SOE agent, Violette Szabo, on 24 March 1944, as a tool in encrypting messages. It stands as her epitaph.

Violette Reine Elizabeth Szabo (née Bushell) was born in Paris on 26 June 1921, the daughter of Charles George Bushell, who was British, and Reine Blanche Leroy, who was French. Her father moved them to Brixton in 1932 and he started a car dealership. Violette went to a school in the Stockwell Road until she was fourteen when she left to take a job on the perfume counter of a shop. On 21 August 1940, after a very brief courtship beginning on Bastille Day (14 July), the strikingly beautiful

Violette married Etienne Renée Szabo a French-Hungarian who had already fought in Norway against the Nazis. He joined de Gaulle's Free French in North Africa and was killed at the battle of El Alamein on 27 October 1942 before he could even see their daughter, Tania, who had been born on 8 June 1941.

Violette, who had already been a member of the Auxiliary Territorial Service since 1941, then decided that she wanted to join the real fight against the Nazis in her husband's place and, because of her knowledge of the French language and France, she was accepted into the SOE in October 1943. She was trained as a 'Bod', in navigation, evasion and escape, use of weapons, self-defence, use of explosives, radio and codes. It was from this time that she enjoyed the reputation of being the best shot in the SOE.

She was dropped twice into occupied France. The first mission was when she parachuted into Cherbourg on 5 April 1944, under codename 'Louise' to assist Philippe Liewer to reassemble the local resistance forces which had recently been decimated by the Germans. Violette also gathered some very useful information about German bomb factories in the area. She then returned, after a successful mission, on 30 April by Lysander airplane (these were small army aircraft which could land and take off on a very short field and were ideal for taking agents to and fro' occupied territory).

On her second mission, Violette was flown to Limoges on the night of 7–8 June 1944, right after D-Day, in order to disrupt German communications in their attempt to repulse the allied landings. Unfortunately, a German Waffen SS major (Sturmbannführer Helmut Kämpfe) had been kidnapped by the local resistance and, as he was the highest ranking officer that the resistance had ever captured, there was a concentrated search for him, involving snap roadblocks and much brutality.

At midday on 10 June 1944, Violette and two companions were in a car at Salon-la-Tour, outside Limoges, when they were stopped at a roadblock.

Exactly what happened after the car carrying Violette was stopped or why the occupants should especially arouse so much suspicion is not clear. The most famous version of the turn of events is that there was a fierce gun battle with Violette and her Sten gun covering the retreat of her colleagues through the standing corn and then running out of ammunition before being arrested. But Vera Atkins of the SOE was of the view that Violette had tripped and fallen and been arrested unarmed. Yet another version (mentioned below), has Violette defending her position in a building until running out of ammunition. In any event, it appears that her colleagues did escape.

That same afternoon, a division of the SS massacred six hundred and fifty civilians in the nearby village of Oradour-sur-Glane.

Violette was put in the custody of the SS in Limoges, where she was interrogated for four days. After that, she went to Fresnes Prison in Paris and then to the Gestapo HQ at 84 Avenue Foch, where she was further interrogated and tortured. Having given nothing except her contempt, on 8 August, she was put on a train bound for Germany. On board, she crawled around dispensing water to fellow prisoners while the train was being attacked by the RAF. At Ravensbrück concentration camp she was assigned to hard labour with her colleagues Lilian Rolfe and Denise Bloch at Torgau.

They were then sent to a punishment camp at Klein Königsberg, and emerged severely debilitated. In late January or early February 1945 they were taken back to Ravensbrück where they were murdered by shooting and their bodies were cremated in the camp crematorium.

The citation for Violette's George Cross appeared in the *London Gazette* on 17 December 1946 and George VI presented the award to four year old Tania in 1946, explaining to her that, as it was her mother's award, Tania should wear it on the right hand side of her breast, in her mother's memory.

'THE KING has been graciously pleased to award the GEORGE CROSS to: —

Violette, Madame SZABO (deceased), Women's Transport Service (First Aid Nursing Yeomanry).

Madame Szabo volunteered to undertake a particularly dangerous mission in France. She was parachuted into France in April, 1944, and undertook the task with enthusiasm. In her execution of the delicate researches entailed she showed great presence of mind and astuteness. She was twice arrested by the German security authorities but each time managed to get away. Eventually, however, with other members of her group, she was surrounded by the Gestapo in a house in the south west of France. Resistance appeared hopeless but Madame Szabo, seizing a Sten gun and as much ammunition as she could carry, barricaded herself in part of the house and, exchanging shot for shot with the enemy, killed or wounded several of them. By constant movement, she avoided being cornered and fought until she dropped exhausted. She was arrested and had to undergo solitary confinement.

She was then continuously and atrociously tortured but never by word or deed gave away any of her acquaintances or told the enemy anything of any value. She was ultimately executed. Madame Szabo gave a magnificent example of courage and steadfastness.'

Violette was also awarded the Croix de Guerre by France and the MBE. Surviving fellow SOE agent Odette Sansom Hallowes (Churchill) GC said of Violette in the year 2000: 'She was the bravest of us all.' A film called *Carve Her Name With Pride* was made about Violette in 1958, and in 2009 a bust of her was unveiled on the Albert Embankment opposite Lambeth Palace, as a memorial to all SOE agents. Of the fifty-five female agents, thirteen were killed in action or perished in a concentration camp.

Chapter 26

A Note on the Present and the Future

'Then imitate the action of the tiger;
Stiffen the sinews, summon up the blood.'

From Act III, scene I of *Henry V*
by William Shakespeare

BRITONS ARE still adventurers. It must be something in the sea air or in the blood of our island race. Modern greats include Sir Ranulph Fiennes, who is, according to the *Guinness Book of Records*, 'The world's greatest living explorer' after his 100,000 mile transglobe expedition in 1982. Sir Chris Bonington, after over fifty years of climbing, is still at it. Sir Robin Knox-Johnston was the first man to sail solo and non-stop around the world. Colonel John Blashford-Snell, in his Norton & Sons 'explorer suits', typifies the eccentric English adventurer. However, his descent of the Blue Nile in 1968 and exploration of the Congo River in the mid-1970s were tremendous achievements and popularised white-water rafting. He also founded Operation Raleigh to give youngsters a taste of adventure. Sir Chay Blyth first came to notice for rowing the Atlantic in 1966 and then became the first man to sail the wrong way round the world. Kenton Cool famously climbed (with Ian Parnell), Annapuma III in Nepal and has been on top of the world six times, including twice in the same week. Richard Meredith-Hardy is twice winner of the Britannia Trophy and the only man ever to have flown a microlight aircraft over the summit of Mount Everest. Brian Milton once drove right across the Sahara and became the first man to microlight around the world. Despite Richard Branson's attempts (but let us also note him in passing), Brian Jones and Bertrand Piccard became the first men to pilot a balloon non-stop around the world. Rick Stanton is a noted underwater cave explorer. In 2007 Justine Curgenven took her kayak the one thousand and seven hundred miles around New Zealand's South Island. Roz Savage has rowed solo across the Atlantic and from California to Hawaii. Dee Caffari was the first woman to sail solo the wrong way around the world. Jason Lewis spent thirteen years pedalling around the world, and Pen Hadow is the only man ever to have trekked solo to the North Pole from Canada. Benedict Allen has explored Amazonia, Papua New Guinea and the Namib Desert, introducing the world to the contemporaneous video-diary in the process. Dame Ellen MacArthur's 2005, record-breaking, solo circumnavigation brought her international renown and, in accordance with the traditions of Sir Francis Drake and Sir Francis Chichester (after their epic circumnavigations), the immediate award of a DBE at the age of twenty-nine. She is probably the youngest ever recipient, and far more deserving than the football managers and pop singers on whom these awards are far too casually conferred (indeed, like the confetti that Nehru condemned!).

Bibliography

Abbott, General Sir James; *Narrative of A Journey from Heraut to Khiva, Moscow and St Petersburgh* (1856, 2nd edition).

Allen, Alexandra; *Travelling Ladies* (Jupiter, 1980).

Archer, Jeffrey; *Paths of Glory* (Macmillan, 2009).

Aylward, Gladys and Christine Hunter; *The Little Woman* (Moody Press, 1995).

Bell, Gertrude; *Safar Nameh* (Cambridge University Press, 2011); *Poems from the Divan of Hafiz* (Dodo Press, 2008); *The Thousand and One Churches* (University of Pennsylvania, 2008); *Amurath to Amurath* (Juniper Grove, 2008); *The Palace and Mosque of Ukhaidir* (BiblioBazaar, 2009); *The Desert and the Sown* (Dover Publications, 2009).

Birkett, Dea; *Mary Kingsley: Imperial Adventuress* (Palgrave Macmillan, 1992).

Burgess, Alan; *The Small Woman* (Reprint Society Bookclub, 1959).

Chichester, Sir Francis; *Gipsy Moth Circles the World* (Stodder & Houghton, 1967).

Colenso, John William; *The Pentateuch and The Book of Joshua Critically Examined* (Colenso, 1862).

Dictionary of National Biography (Oxford University Press, revised on-line edition).

Fawcett, Col P. H. and Fawcett, Brian; *Exploration Fawcett* (Book Club edition, 1954).

Fielding, Xan; *Hide and Seek: The Story of A Wartime Agent* (Secker & Warburg, 1954).

Fisher, John; *That Miss Hobhouse* (Martin Secker & Warburg, 1971).

Fleming, (Robert) Peter; *A Brazilian Adventure* (Reprint Society Edition, 1933); *Travels in Tartary* (Jonathan Cape, 1941).

French, Patrick; *Younghusband: The Last Great Imperial Adventurer* (Harper Perennial, 1994).

Geniesse, J. F; *Passionate Nomad: The Life of Freya Stark* (Modern Library, 1999).

Geographical Journal 68.4 1926: 363–368 (Obituary of Gertrude Bell, by D. G. Hogarth).

Gillies, Midge; *Queen of the Air* (Phoenix, 2009).

Hall, John; *That Bloody Woman: The Turbulent Life of Emily Hobhouse* (Truran Books, 2008).

Haslip, Joan; *Lady Hester Stanhope* (History Press ed. 2006).

Holzel, Tom and Sakeld, Audrey; *The Mystery of Mallory and Irvine* (Pimlico, 3rd revised ed. 1999).

Johnson, Amy; *Sky Roads of The World* (W & R Chambers, 1939).

Jones, Liane; *A Quiet Courage* (Corgi, 1990).

Kingsley, Mary; *Travels in West Africa* (Macmillan, 1897); *West African Studies* (Macmillan, 1899).

Lempriere, J.; *Lempriere's Classical Dictionary* (Bracken Books, 1984).

Leslie, Anita; *Francis Chichester* (Hodder & Stoughton, 1975).

Mackay, James A.; *The Man Who Invented Himself: The Life of Sir Thomas Lipton* (Mainstream, 1998).

Maclean, Fitzroy; *Eastern Approaches* (Jonathan Cape, 1949).

Mahabharata, The (Penguin Classics, 2001).

Masson, Madeleine; *Christine: A Search For Christine Granville GM, OBE Croix de Guerre* (Hamish Hamilton, 1975).

National Archives [File HS 9/612].

Norgay, Tenzing; (with James Ramsey) *Man of Everest* (Gibson Square, 2010); (with Malcolm Barnes) *After Everest* (Allen & Unwin, 1977).

Quiller-Couch, Sir Arthur; *From a Cornish Window* (Cambridge University Press, 1928).

Ramayana, The (Penguin Classics, 1977).

Rowse, A. L.; *The Controversial Colensos* (Truran, 1989).

Russell, W. H.; *The War* (Routledge, 1856).

St John, Sir Spenser; *The Life of Sir James Brooke, Rajah of Sarawak* (originally published in 1879, reprinted by OUP, 1994).

Seacole, Mary; *The Wonderful Adventures of Mrs Seacole in Many Lands* (James Blackwood, 1857).

Stark, Freya; *The Valley of The Assassins* (New Edition edition, 2001); *Perseus in the Wind; Traveller's Prelude; Ionia; Alexander's Path* (Century edition, 1984); *Beyond the Euphrates* (John Murray, 1951); *The Coast of Incense* (John Murray, 1953); *Dust in the Lion's Paw* (John Murray, 1961).

Tregellas, W. H.; *Cornish Worthies* (1884 reprint by Kessinger Publishing, 2008).

Trevelyan, G. M.; *Garibaldi and the Thousand* (London, 1908); Garibaldi and the Making of Italy (London, 1911).

Wright, Thomas; *The Life of Sir Richard Burton* (G. P. Putnam & Sons, 1906).

Newspapers and Periodicals

The Daily Telegraph; Obituaries, various.
The Guardian; Obituaries, various.
The Independent; Obituaries, various.
The London Gazette; various.
The Scotsman; Obituary for Fitzroy Maclean.
The Times; Obituaries, various.
The Times of India; Obituary for Tenzing Norgay.
The West Briton; 29 April 1864.
The New York Times; various.